The Complete Book of

TEDDY BEAR ARTISTS

In Australia & New Zealand

The Complete Book of

TEDDY BEAR ARTISTS

In Australia & New Zealand

A Who's Who of Bear Artists in the Antipodes

Jennifer Laing

SALLY MILNER PUBLISHING

*In loving memory of Pat Lovelock, one of
Australia's first and best loved bear artists.*

The old and the new.
*Henry, a 1909 bear by Steiff, sits with Geoffrey, a bear made by the
author. Watercolour painting also by the author.*

First published in 1996 by
Sally Milner Publishing
RMB 54 Burra Road
Burra Creek NSW 2620 Australia

© Jennifer Laing, 1995

Design by Pereira Design
Film by Wellmak, Hong Kong
Printed by South China Printing,
Hong Kong

Laing, Jennifer, 1954-
 The complete book of teddy bear
artists in Australia and New Zealand

ISBN 1 86351 189 X

1. Teddy bears. 2. Teddy bear
makers - Australia - Directories. 3.
Teddy bear makers - New Zealand -
Directories. I. Title.

745.592402594

Photograph on page 2 shows early work
of founding members of the
Antipodean Bear-makers Co-op.

Contents

Foreword

ENNIFER LAING IS one of the world's foremost teddy bear artists. Not only is her work of the high quality we have come to admire in the genre of handmade bears, but she also cherishes the closeness of the teddy bear community, and the sense of co-operation and camaraderie that these unique artists share with each other and the public.

Personally, the rewards of involvement in the artist bear world continue to bring great satisfaction to me. I especially enjoy my association with the talented artists who create these highly collectable works of art. I deeply admire the artist's creative process as each creator strives to generate an individual expression of joy, wonder and love. As with any fine art, some of these expressions may be more fiscally valuable than others, and the final judgement of clear-cut values is yet to be established in this art form.

The availability of fabrics and supplies plays an enormous part in the growth of this artistic expression. Aside from changes in patterns, sizes or positioning of eyes and ears, there has been one major catalyst for a seemingly endless variety of characters that have come upon the scene since 1984. Introducing the teddy bear artist to mohair in the form of yardage was like introducing an artist to a colour palette; it unleashed a creativity that has stretched the imagination beyond belief.

The bears depicted in this book are but a few examples of this extraordinary art form. I am honoured to introduce these pages to you, just as I have been proud to include some of the best known Australian artists in my San Diego Teddy Bear, Doll and Antique Toy Show and Sale.

There is, among bear artists, a tremendous sense of sharing and support, which adds to the ongoing popularity and growth of bear-making. One important factor in this warm sense of unity is books such as this.

Linda Mullins

Introduction

TEDDY BEARS SEEM to strike a deep chord in many people around the world. Ever since their 'evolution' and first appearance around 1903, teddy bears have lived in our homes and in our hearts. A teddy bear was often our first friend and confidant. Our bears have grown up with us and in many cases have remained with us throughout life's journey, symbolising love and security, loyalty and trust.

Right from the start, a teddy was more than a baby's toy. It was terribly fashionable for ladies to be seen carrying one or to have a small bear pinned to a coat as a lapel ornament. Bears made appearances at weddings and social events. President 'Teddy' Roosevelt used them as both table decorations at dinner parties and gifts on his campaign trail. Teddy bears were the first manufactured toy to become a worldwide instant hit, and their popularity has never waned.

Teddy bear collecting is said to have its roots in the 1920s and was especially popular in the United States, where the first fan clubs, specialist magazines and shops appeared. In England and Europe, the collecting bug only really bit in the 1960s, when the English actor and personality Peter Bull was instrumental in bringing teddy bears and their lovers out of the closets.

Collectors of old bears are now finding that vintage teddies are becoming increasingly scarce and more expensive, with record auction prices of $55,000, $110,000 and $250,000 being reached for old Steiff bears in the last few years. However, not all old bears have impeccable pedigrees and are worth such princely sums, and not all collectors desire only the vintage or the rare.

A growing number of collectors, finding the old bears too expensive for their budgets, are turning to a relatively new teddy bear phenomenon, that of the artist bear. These special bears are made by talented individual craftspeople usually working from home. Their unique designs and interpretation of the teddy bear often began from the desire to re-create the quality and character found in the early bears, or perhaps in their own childhood bear. Personal styles, looks and characters have evolved in these bears. Each bear is often one-of-a-kind or made as part of a very small edition, guaranteeing a specialness that is missing in the mass-produced bear.

What began in the early 1970s on the west coast of the United States with a handful of bear-makers has now become a worldwide movement. Solo bear-makers are breathing new life into the teddy bear, and their creations are highly sought after by collectors the world over. These artistic creators of the modern handmade teddy bear are called 'teddy bear artists', a term first coined by Carol-Lynn Rossel-Waugh (herself a bear artist) in 1984.

Teddy bear artists are rare and talented people who are able to satisfy their creative urges by making not just objects of beauty, but little creatures who almost have a life of their own, and who can inspire love and all those warm emotions from our childhood. Bear artists are often adept in many different areas, such as visualising, drawing, designing and sewing, as well as being proficient in a number of mediums, such as textiles, wood, clay, porcelain, metals and resins. Each artist is working on his or her personal vision of the ideal teddy bear, and as the artist's ideas change so we can see the evolution reflected in the artist's work.

This constantly changing and dynamic world of the bear artists makes it a very exciting one for teddy bear collectors. New artists are continually appearing and establishing themselves. The best of these become world-famous and continue

to demonstrate the originality and imagination that made the bear artist so popular in the first place.

Bear artists first appeared in Australia and New Zealand in the 1980s, and conditions were possibly tougher for us here than anywhere else. The first handful of bear-makers were frustrated in that they were working alone, without contact with their peers, and there were no supplies of quality fabrics available in the southern hemisphere. There were no books available on the subject of making quality bears and no classes from which to learn. These professional artists learned the hard way and often had to import their materials themselves.

In 1991 all that changed when a group of 12 full-time bear artists got together and founded The Antipodean Bear-makers Co-op, the first organisation of its kind in Australia and New Zealand. This network was designed to bring together bear artists to share ideas, solve problems, obtain supplies more easily, provide a support group and make friends. The original concept was formed by Jennifer Laing (Totally Bear) of Sydney, and the name was given to the group by Michael and Judy Walton (An Original Teddy) of New Zealand. The first members were Winifred Belmont, Loris Hancock, June Kittlety, Jennifer Laing, Cindy Lowe, Pat Lovelock, Briony Nottage, Jenny Round, Pat Tomlinson, Kay Vanderley, Michael and Judy Walton, and Gerry Warlow. From the nucleus of 13 founding members, the Co-op now has over 100 professional bear artists in its ranks, including many whose work is known, loved and collected around the world.

The growth of the Co-op alone indicates the interest in artist bears in our small corner of the world. Clubs, organisations, shops, magazines and shows dedicated to bears both old and new are springing up all over Australia and New Zealand. In late 1994 Australia held its first truly international all-bear show, the First Sydney International Bear Fair, and showed the world what talent we have here in our midst.

That is also the aim of this book. There are so many aspects to the magical world of teddy bears, and artist bears are forming an increasingly larger part of it. The bears you see here are made by individual men and women, by friends working together, by sisters working with each other, and by husbands and wives working as a team. Different aims and ideals motivate each artist. Some intend from the outset to set up a commercial enterprise and to produce quality bears in fairly large numbers, while others are not concerned with a large output. Some are not only committed to producing each bear themselves but sometimes even insist on hand-stitching every seam.

Whatever their aims, each bear artist is working hard to create the best bears he or she is capable of, and it is exciting to see the breadth of talent emerging from our corner of the planet. One of our artists, Judi Newman of Queensland, sums it up very well:

'Bear-making has been my window to opportunity. Through bears I have travelled, collected, taught, practised art and sewed. All I have loved and worked for is wrapped up in the teddy bear. It allows me the freedom to run my own business. Giving is also a nice part of bear-making. The teddy bear business is a culmination of all that I am.'

Being able to make a living from doing something you love and from something you have personally created is one of the most satisfying things you can achieve in life. If that is what you want to do, no matter what field it is in, you have to give it all you have, and make your opportunities. Perseverance is important, as is self-motivation, because there will be long hours, loneliness and frustrations. But achieving something all by yourself can do wonders for your confidence, and most of us could do with more of this commodity.

The imagination and skills of over 70 very different bear artists shine here for the world to see, and I hope you will enjoy the results of all their hard work.

A family group of Katherine's bears, all in mohair with suede paws and glass eyes.

KATHERINE ALAM

Bondi Beach Bears

KATHERINE HAS MADE soft toys for most of her life, and so it seemed a natural progression to work on bears. She made her first 'real' bears in 1993 and they quickly sold through a local shop. A Certificate in Fine Arts from the National Art College honed her artistic talents.

Although she only works at her bears part-time, as she is also a midwife, Katherine puts a lot of effort into every bear and does all the work herself. She makes about 35 bears a year, and all are one-offs or limited editions, each being defined as 'unique, handcrafted, hand-sewn and almost alive'. She prefers to work on smaller bears, from 20 cm (8") to 25 cm (10") in size. Bondi Beach Bears are identified by a small sewn-in label, and are sold in both wholesale and retail outlets. Following her own muse, Katherine works on constantly improving her designs and gets great enjoyment from her work. Her biggest satisfaction is in seeing each bear become a little creature as it is created, and she finds it hard to part with them all.

Katherine regards bear-making as an artistic pursuit not unlike sculpture, and her advice to anyone with an artistic bent is this: if you want to create your own lovable little creatures, start making teddy bears!

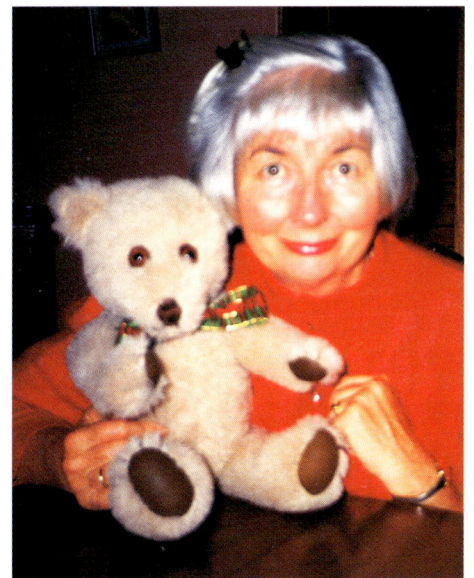

Katherine with Howie, made from Australian wool as a replica of a 1954 bear for the owner's 40th birthday.

3

LINDA BENSON

Benson Bears

LINDA WAS ABOUT 16 when she made her first bear, but she is not sure what inspired her to start. She does not remember having a bear as a child and says that perhaps that is why, but even as a bear artist she still does not have one! Brought up in a family of craftspeople, Linda says that all four of her siblings have inherited a creative urge. 'As kids, if we weren't creating, Mum and Dad thought we were sick!' Linda's creativity led her to complete a Diploma of Art in Textiles, as 'the "tactility" of textiles has always appealed'.

Max (left), 38 cm (15"), in English mohair with ultrasuede paws, bootbutton eyes, poly/pellet/buckshot-filled; and Robbie, also 38 cm (15"), in German mohair.

Doing all her own work, Linda often works 12 hours a day during the weeks leading up to a show. Unsure of how many bears she makes, she thinks it must average out to one a day. Her bears range from 2 cm (¾") to 50 cm (20"), with no particular favourite size. They are identified by a hand-embroidered ribbon tag, which simply reads 'Benson', sewn into the back seam.

Linda sees the bears she makes today as having a more intelligent look than those she made a few years ago. 'There's something in their eyes. They seem more "real" now, less toylike'. She loves looking at catalogues and fur samples and finds that often a fabric will suggest a new pattern. Linda's bears are quality bears, and each is a traditionally styled, handcrafted original.

Benson Bears are sold wholesale to shops and by Linda at shows, where she enjoys meeting bear lovers. Linda also teaches bear-making classes.

Marcus (left), 40 cm (16"), in German mohair and recycled jumper with bootbutton eyes; and little Rafferty, 21 cm (8¼"), in English mohair with glass eyes. Both have buckshot added for extra weight.

Little Sam and Benny, 13 cm (5") in German mohair with hand-smocked outfits and leather shoes. Sam has a new cardigan and Benny has a wooden car.

4

Morgan, 35 cm (14"), in curly German mohair with safety eyes.

Edward, 29 cm (11½"), in crushed mohair with glass eyes, pellet-filled.

SIMONE BURKE

Bears by Simone

A LOVE OF BEARS must run in the blood in Simone's family, as her mother owns a delightful bear shop called Aussie Bear in the historic Sydney area, The Rocks, and has collected bears for many years. Simone has worked in the shop since 1986, and naturally she is a collector and bear lover herself, with over 200 bears living in her house.

Simone started making bears in 1991, but her first bears were not sold

Simone with Albert.

until 1993, when she had completed an architectural drafting certificate as well as an interior design diploma. Still working at Aussie Bear, Simone is currently making bears part-time. She enjoys experimenting with new fabrics and developing new patterns. Most of her bears are one-offs, as she likes them to have their own personality, although she has done a limited edition of 10 as well as one of 25 pieces.

All Bears by Simone have a green and gold fabric label stitched into their back, along with a swing tag bearing their name, date of birth, materials used and signature. Simone presently wholesales to several stores as well as selling her bears from home.

Simone attended the First Sydney International Bear Fair at Darling Harbour in 1994 and is looking forward to doing more shows in 1995.

DEE GLOSSOP

Dee Glossop Teddy Bears & Accessories

Monty, 33 cm (13"), in soft synthetic with glass eyes. Also available in kit form.

the-line Australian fashion boutiques. It seemed a natural progression to her to start designing and making her own line of teddy bears. The bear-making has in turn led to Dee and her husband, Doug, opening their own bear-making supply business in Sydney.

As well as being busy with her supply business, Dee is a tutor with the NSW Government's Diversional Therapy programs at correctional centres, where she teaches bear-making to prisoners. Initially nervous at the prospect, Dee was amazed at how gentle and responsive her pupils were. 'We have quite a number of mail-order customers in Long Bay, Berrima and other jails who are now making magnificent teddy bears and I would highly recommend these bears to collectors.' Dee is pleased to be able to contribute to the development of the creative skills of those who may not otherwise have had the opportunity.

Dee's bears are easily recognised by their distinctive thumbs and tails, as well as by a leatherette tag sewn into the seam near the tail.

A MOTHER OF FIVE, Dee cannot remember a time when she was not busy sewing and creating things. Most of her early business career was spent designing and manufacturing garments for top-of-

Dee holding Seymour, 38 cm (15"), a limited edition of six, in distressed mohair with bootbutton eyes and cotton stuffing.

Timothy, 50 cm (20"), a yes/no bear in mohair. Dee also sells three sizes of the yes/no mechanism.

RHONDA HARLAND

Booalbyn Bears

RHONDA HAD AN unusual introduction to the world of bear-making in March 1992. 'Because of my agoraphobia, my mother-in-law took me to a bear-making class. As I was already collecting bears, she thought it would help me overcome my fears of going out, and maybe give me a new interest.' It certainly did give her an interest, and within a few months Rhonda was selling her own bears at shows.

Rhonda now works on her bear-making full-time, 'except when the housework interrupts me'. She finds that she makes 80-100 bears a year, with her output increasing. She enjoys working alone on her bears, as she says it gives her control over the style and quality and makes the bears' characters totally hers. Most of her work is one-offs, although she has completed a limited edition of 25 little 15 cm (6") bears in flower pots. Her favourite size is a 38 cm (15") bear, but she enjoys the challenge of making bears from 15 cm (6") to 70 cm (28") also.

Rhonda's traditionally styled mohair bears are sometimes dressed, and she has occasionally ventured into designing coloured bears to suit people's home decor. Her ideal bear is one that makes a person feel warm and cuddly inside, and she is rapidly realising her aim of taking her bears from the realm of soft toys to that of collectable heirlooms. Boalbyn Bears can be identified by a ceramic disc bearing their trade name worn around their necks.

Rhonda manages about three shows a year and gains immense satisfaction in seeing people taking Boalbyn Bears off to loving new homes. Her bears have done well at show competitions and have also appeared in national bear

(Group) Rhonda's Early Australian Series of 38 cm (15") dressed bears in mohair. Includes a farming couple and a swagman.

magazines, and Rhonda teaches bear-making in small classes from her home. If you are interested in bear-making, Rhonda believes you should 'go to as many shows as you can, take as many bear-making classes as you can, read as much as you can on bears, and talk to as many people as you can, because you can never learn enough'.

Rhonda with big Sebastian and Oliver, both in mohair with leather pawpads and bootbutton eyes. Sebastian has a centre seam and Oliver is olive, both a little different!

LEXIE HAWORTH

Bears of Haworth Cottage

'I made my first teddy bear in June 1992 after attending a local doll and bear show. It was the first time I had seen artist bears and I was very impressed with the variety of styles. I had always loved teddies and old toys and still have my own bear, an Alpha Farnell circa 1948.'

Lexie with Merrick, 61 cm (24"), in German mohair with felt paws, glass eyes and poly/pellet stuffing. An open-edition bear.

Poor Bear, 61 cm (24"), in 'antiqued' German mohair with felt paws, glass eyes and poly/pellet stuffing. A one-of-a-kind.

McDougal (with appropriate tartan scarf), 40 cm (16"), in German mohair with mohair reversed pawpads, glass eyes and poly/pellet stuffing, together with his smaller Poor Bear friend.

(Left) Merrick with his larger friend Worland, also in mohair, signed and numbered on his foot.

Within a few months Lexie was selling her own bears at her first Mittagong show, run by Heather Brook, who has shown Lexie much encouragement and friendship. Lexie is still amazed that she is earning a living from making bears. She showed great artistic promise as a teenager but, regretfully, didn't follow a career in the arts because of family reasons. Now she feels she has been given a second chance, as she finds that bear-making more than fulfils her need to express herself creatively.

Although she creates her bears herself, often putting in 12–14 hour days, her daughter-in-law helps with the book-work and other time-consuming tasks. Lexie produces about 200 bears a year, and they are mostly one-of-a-kinds with some limited editions and open editions. She likes to work on bears ranging from 56 cm (22") to 60 cm (24"). Each of Lexie's bears has a tag sewn into the back seam and a signed and detailed swing tag. Her bears are mostly sold through shops or at the three or four shows she attends each year.

Lexie has won prizes in competitions and has appeared in Australian and English bear magazines, but she con-siders her finest achievement to be the appearance of her bear Worland on the cover of *Bear Facts Review* magazine. She also felt honoured when Paul and Rosemary Volpp, American bear collectors, and well-known owners of the famous old Steiff bear "Happy", added one of her Aboriginal bears to their collection.

'My wish is that Australian bear artists can remain a closely knit group and that they continue to encourage one another in their pursuits. The last three years have been very exciting for me. My bear-making has opened up a new life for my husband and me. Every day there's a new challenge.'

SHARON HELLEUR

Blue Mountain Bears

ON A TRIP TO England in 1989 Sharon was given two old bears by relatives, and this sparked her interest in the world of bears. After reading an article about Karla Mahanna, she took up the challenge to try to create her own bear. Because of illness, however, this was not possible until 1992, when Sharon made her first bear – 'and he was a disaster!'. Nevertheless she persevered, and within a year was selling her bears at local markets.

Sharon's main frustration is that the medication she needed in 1990, when she was diagnosed with Hodgkin's disease, has affected the use of her hands, sometimes making it impossible to work. However, she still manages to make about 150 bears a year, and what started for her as a form of therapy has become a lifeline. 'I don't look too far into the future, and as long as I enjoy making bears and they continue to make other people happy, I will continue.'

While Sharon works alone on her bears, her husband makes the joint discs and her mother-in-law knits the bears' jumpers. Most of the bears are one-offs with the occasional limited edition of no more than 15. Sharon's bears are robust characters, many able to stand unaided, others pellet-filled and poseable. They all have a sewn-in label in the back as well as a swing tag.

Sharon is intrigued by the wide range of people who buy a bear for themselves. 'I once sold a bear to a businessman, as he wanted a small bear to travel with him in his briefcase. A member of a motorcycle gang also bought one!'

The Colonel, 40 cm (16″) in distressed mohair with suede paws, glass eyes and handmade glasses.

Sharon with Chelsea, made from mohair with felt pawpads and glass eyes.

A hug of Blue Mountain Bears, including Grandpa with glasses and stick, a 1994 Sydney Royal Easter Show winner.

Sunny (right) and Jonquil, 48 cm (19") and 30 cm (12"), both in German mohair and wearing hand-knitted wool outfits. Sunny has bent limbs with poseable armature.

JAN HOBART

Gaza Grizzlies

A LOVE OF BEARS inspired her, and Jan's creative curiosity spurred her on to master yet another skill in making bears. Jan was already involved in other crafts, notably knitwear designing. She made her first bear in October 1993 and within a year was selling her work professionally, first at the Sydney International Bear Fair in 1994 where she was pleased with her success.

Working full-time on her bears, Jan makes around 50 a year. She creates all of the bears' exclusive hand-knits and designs and works their embroidery. Some of her Gaza Grizzlies are open editions and some are one-offs, and her favourite size is between 25 cm (10") and 30 cm (12"). Jan works only with German mohair and favours the curly varieties. The bears all have an embroidered label sewn into the back seam as well as a swing card with her Eucalyptus logo on the front and a description inside. Jan's Gaza Grizzlies are available wholesale and retail.

'My husband and son do not appear to have any interest in my bears but, curiously, in my absence, the bears seem to come to life and move into all sorts of unusual positions. They can be found lounging around, standing on their heads and hanging off the ceiling fans.'

Jan enjoys all aspects of bear-making and encourages newcomers to experiment with their own designs, as she believes there is nothing as rewarding as creating something that is all your own.

Jan Hobart

MENA JOHNSON

IN 1988 MENA CAME across a book on mini felt bears and spent all one Sunday making her first. From then on she was hooked, and in 1993 started selling her little bears through a local gift shop.

Having completed an Advanced Commercial Needlecraft Certificate and dabbled in many crafts in the past, Mena now works full-time on her bears, producing over 250 a year. She does not have any assistance in her work. Ranging between 4 cm (1½'') and 7.5 cm (3''), her bears have a tiny ultrasuede tag in the back seam with 'MJ' on it and a swing card. They are sold through both wholesale and retail outlets, and have won several prizes in competitions. Mena also teaches miniature bear-making classes and attends up to six shows a year.

Sukie, 9 cm (3½''), in German mohair, with The Keeper and Quentin, both under 7 cm (2¾''), and red Christabelle, 4 cm (1½'').

Mena Johnson

Benson, a saggy pellet-filled bear, Rosebud, Santa and Panda. All between 5 cm (2'') and 9 cm (3½'').

With miniatures, Mena has found that 'very fine stitching is vitally important as there is no room for error. Also, what is satisfactory in jointing a 7.5 cm (3'') bear is not necessarily going to work on a 4 cm (1½'') bear'.

Mena hopes to travel overseas with her bears and just wishes that there were more hours in the day for her bear-making. She feels that with time her bears are becoming more distinctive and more alive with character.

LORRAINE KEEN

Individual Bears

Belvedere (front), 28 cm (11"), in German mohair, with glass eyes, wool stuffing and bells in his belly; and Howard (in trunk), his bigger brother at 38 cm (15"), who is pellet-filled.

LORRAINE DECIDED ON a change of career and chose bear-making in 1993. After a successful start at a local show she decided to pursue it further. She found her training in draughting helpful when designing new patterns, and occasionally her daughter assists with the faces. 'I love to leave the eyes and noses to last, thus making the bear come alive. I find it hard to work on a bear while it is looking at me!' Lorraine's Individual Bears have printed labels in the left leg seam and a swing tag giving their details.

Working part-time in a sales position, Lorraine spends two days a week on her bears and still manages to make around 200 bears a year, mostly as one-offs. She sells mainly to shops and has received orders for her bears from as far afield as the United States. Lorraine also teaches bear-making at a local college.

In the near future Lorraine would like bear-making to become a full-time project. 'In later years I would like to retire with my family to the country and run a "Bear Barn" where I can not only make bears but run workshops and open to the public.'

Lorraine with Oscar, 50 cm (20"), a yes/no bear in German mohair with glass eyes and wool stuffing.

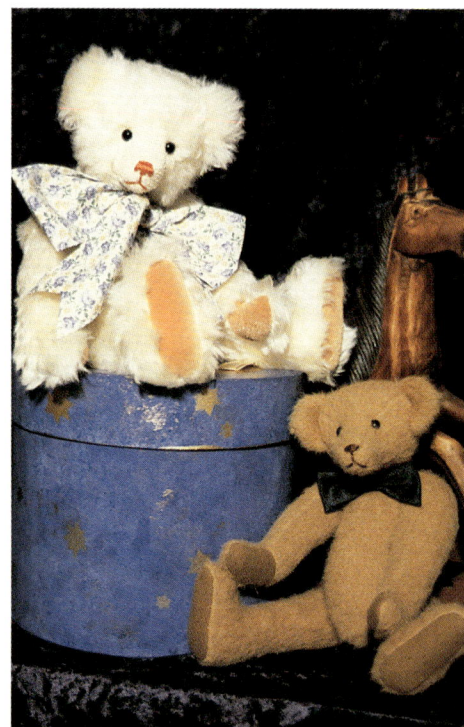

Belle, 38 cm (15"), in white German mohair with glass eyes, wool stuffing and bells in her belly; and Oswald, 28 cm (11"), in alpaca with glass eyes, polyfill stuffing and a bow tie.

12

A group of Shirley's smaller bears.

SHIRLEY KERR

Penny Bears

A BEAR LOVER AND collector for over 20 years, Shirley never dreamed that one day she would be making her own bears. But after taking lessons with Jennifer Laing in 1992 she was hooked. After years of being involved in various crafts, from painting, patchwork and pottery, to china-painting and making porcelain dolls, Shirley discovered that her true love is bear-making.

When she first started making bears, Shirley couldn't bring herself to part with them, in spite of Jennifer repeatedly saying how good they were and how well they would sell. Now, after making over 130 of them, Shirley is more able to part with them and collectors are delighted to purchase her sweet and special little bears.

Every Penny Bear is a one-of-a-kind, and each is entirely hand-stitched. They all have names and a small leather tag in their back seam with Shirley's initials, 'SK', and the year she made them.

Shirley has been seriously ill over the last few years and has found that bear-making has been great therapy, especially sewing by hand. Her bears recently won three prizes at the International Bear Fair at Darling Harbour, Sydney.

Shirley with Ben, Buffy and Angus. All Shirley's bears are one-offs in mohair.

Mary, 25 cm (10"), in beige with a lace collar, Wendell, 35 cm (14"), in honey, and little Ben, 22 cm (8¾"), in distressed beige. (Wendell and Ben are also featured on the front cover.)

13

JENNIFER LAING

Totally Bear

ALTHOUGH FASCINATED with the variety and artistry of bear-makers around the world, Jennifer's true passion has always been old Steiffs. 'They have been through so much and seen so much that they have somehow absorbed something of life itself. They have developed strength of character in a different way from the modern artist bears, with love and adventure over time.'

A professional artist who also has a degree in science, Jennifer first turned to bear-making in 1990. Dismayed at the poor quality of and lack of 'life' in many modern mass-produced bears, Jennifer set out to make her own style of bear in

Jennifer with Benny Long, a limited edition of 25 for Disney World 1994.

the least mass-produced way possible.

She works by herself, only produces bears to individual order and entirely hand-stitches every bear. Each bear is dedicated to its new owner on its swing tag, and also has a small handwritten leather tag in the back seam giving the bear's name and number in the edition, Jennifer's signature and the date. She always works in mohair and, wherever

possible, uses antique bootbuttons for eyes. The editions range from five up to 25, with quite a few prototypes, as Jennifer is constantly adding to her 'archives' of over 60 designs. Sizes range from 10 cm (4") to 46 cm (18"). (The largest was a hand-stitched mohair rocking bear the size of a Shetland pony, a one-of-a-kind for the Disney World Convention 1994.)

Jennifer thinks she makes the plainest bears around, wanting their characters to speak for themselves. Sometimes she does not even put ribbons on them so as not to detract from their 'animal charm'.

Her bears are known around the world and Jennifer was the first bear artist from Australia to be invited to exhibit at the Walt Disney World Teddy Bear Convention in 1993, 1994 and again in 1995. She was also the first to be nominated for a prestigious Golden Teddy Award in 1995. Her bears have appeared on television and in newspapers, books and journals around the world, and have made the covers of both Australian and English bear magazines. Her book and video on bear-making continue to be international best-sellers.

Oskar, a 40 cm (16") polar bear, also from the new Wilderness Series, in a limited edition of 10.

'One of the best aspects of discovering the bear world was being able to become part of a global network of information and friendship. Another was finding out that your initial thoughts of making the perfect bear continually shift and change as your ideas evolve and your bears take on a life of their own. Finally, that I managed to achieve what spurred me on from the start – to make enough from my bears to be able to afford a small collection of ridiculously expensive but completely irresistible old Steiff bears!'

Jennifer is so dedicated to her life with bears that she carries a permanent little travelling bear everywhere she goes; a small teddy bear tattoo!

Grizwald, a 40 cm (16") grizzly bear from Jennifer's new Wilderness Series. A limited edition of 10, in three different sizes to portray a mother, father and cub.

A group of Margaret Ann's Baggage Bears, ready to travel.

MARGARET ANN MANN

Un Petit Bear – The Bear to Wear

MARGARET ANN FIRST thought of making bears when she realised that she needed tenants to live in a $\frac{1}{24}$ scale miniature house she had just built from a kit. She made her first bears in January 1994 and was selling them by March. People were increasingly intrigued by Margaret Ann's little bears, which she wore as brooches, and her work started to sell itself.

Margaret Ann with her bears, both large and small

Although she hasn't had a formal arts education, Margaret Ann has always enjoyed working with her hands and is particularly fond of fine needlework. She currently works on her bears part-time, as she is also an early childhood education teacher and a volunteer Wish Granter for the Starlight Foundation.

Margaret Ann works alone on her bears, which are mostly open editions with some limited editions, and makes around 80 a year. She sells both retail and wholesale. She is justifiably proud of the fact that she has won a medal for her bears at the 1994 First Sydney International Bear Fair, and also for getting the stitches on her bears down to 10-11 to the centimetre ($\frac{3}{8}$").

Margaret Ann says that the size of her bears is 'thumb height and handspan height'. Her tiny 'thumb height' bears are made from suede, ultra-suede, leather and chamois and are hand-buttonhole-stitched from the outside. Each bear is made from 19 separate pieces and has moveable arms and legs. Their eyes are black onyx beads and they all wear a smile. Her handspan Baggage Bears are furry and loose-jointed to fit comfortably into hand luggage, and make great travel companions. Traditionally made from 21

pieces, they are also completely hand-stitched. All of Margaret Ann's bears have a folded logo swing tag or a leather gift tag, and her larger bears have leather tags in the back seam bearing their name and date.

Margaret Ann finds that her bears are evolving over time, developing a more defined snout and a fatter tummy. Her ideal bear, she says, should sit in the hand, have an impish face with smiling eyes and be beautifully made. Her advice is to maintain strict quality control and to love what you are doing, as it really shows in the end product.

'Because my bears are easily transported they are living all over the world. One of my greatest thrills was when 'Brownie' Black Jnr purchased one for his Teddy Bear Museum in Florida, but the story that has given me the greatest pleasure is about the Limited Edition bear that was bought as a present for Linda Mullins. This little bear sits on a coffee table in her living room, and I'm told it is a great conversation piece and much admired.'

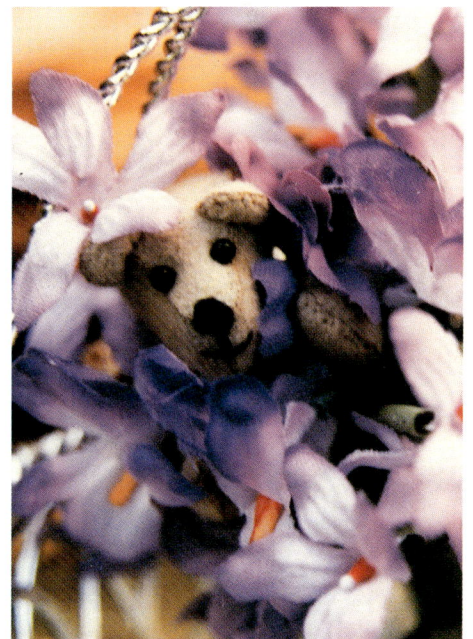

Sweet Violets, 5.5 cm (2$\frac{1}{4}$"), in a flower brooch. Fully jointed, hand-buttonhole-stitched ultrasuede with black onyx eyes.

CAROLE MARSHALL

Balmain Bear

OR CAROLE, THE decision to begin making bears came totally out of the blue. She was ill at the time and was looking for something to do at home, and she had always wanted a bear, ever since hers was swept away in a flood in 1955! She says she only discovered the scope of bear-making after the fact. Carole made her first bear in 1987 and started to sell her bears by word of mouth almost immediately.

With a background in fine arts, Carole still paints, mostly in water-colours, but bear-making has become her full-time occupation. She lavishes care and attention on the personalities of her bears, which are available only in small numbers. They are mostly in small editions of 20 or less, as she likes to experiment with her designs. Balmain Bears are identified by a small woven tag.

Carole is happy to work alone on her bears, but welcomes a break from the solitude occasionally:

A basket of Carole's limited-edition mohair bears, from 30 cm (12") to 40 cm (16").

Old and Scruffy, 30 cm (12") and 23 cm (9"), in antique-style sparse mohair with suede paws and safety eyes. Both are a limited edition of 10 each.

Carole and The Volunteer, 50 cm (20"), in German mohair with suede paws and glass eyes, wearing an old collar, stud and Red Cross pin.

'Bear-making is a solitary occupation and it takes a lot of time, so you tend to get cabin fever. Getting out to shows and talking to collectors on the phone relieves the isolation to a degree, but it is a problem. I know I'm in a bad way, not when I talk to the bears (doesn't everybody?) but when they answer me back.'

A 1993–95 range of Kathleen's bears, from 22 cm (8¾") to 38 cm (15"), all in mohair and all limited editions.

KATHLEEN MASON

Twink Bear Design

ONE BORING SUNDAY afternoon Kathleen paid a chance visit to a local doll show, happened across some beautiful handmade bears and suddenly caught 'the bug'. She made her first bear in early 1993 and began to sell her work several months later, first to friends and then to retail outlets.

Kathleen worked full-time as a computer programmer before bears took over, but she had long been involved in crafts. She now divides her time between part-time secretarial work and bear-making. She is one of the country's youngest bear-makers.

Kathleen finds it difficult to get up the stock for shows because she likes to take her time with her work, and because she is a hand-stitcher. She feels that hand-stitching creates a bear with more personality. 'The more time you spend with each bear, the more personality that is transferred from the maker to the bear. I also believe that bears must be individuals and not mass-produced clones of each other.'

Kathleen makes only about 26 bears a year but each is unique. Her bears range from 5 cm (2") to 38 cm (15"), and she enjoys making all the different sizes. Twink bears can be identified by their labelled and dated leather tags sewn into the back or right underarm seam, as well as their swing tags.

Kathleen's trading name of Twink Bear Design came from the pet name of Twink given to her by her mother because she could twinkle her toes at her when she was in her cot. She still calls her Twink today, sometimes to Kathleen's dismay!

Kathleen and a hug of her bears.

SYLVANA MCAULIFFE

Sylvana's Miniature Bears

SYLVANA'S STORY GOES back to 1979, when on a trip to England she saw Queen Mary's Dollhouse and was inspired by the perfection of the miniatures. Upon returning home she started work on nursery accessories for her own version of a doll's house. Copying her children's toys in miniature, Sylvana attempted her first little bear, all 4 cm (1½") of him. She still has him to remind her of her beginnings in bear-making.

A range of Sylvana's bears made over the last six years, ranging from 4 cm (1½") to 10 cm (4"). The bear in a lavender dress is a potpourri and the one in white lace and bonnet is a two-faced bear.

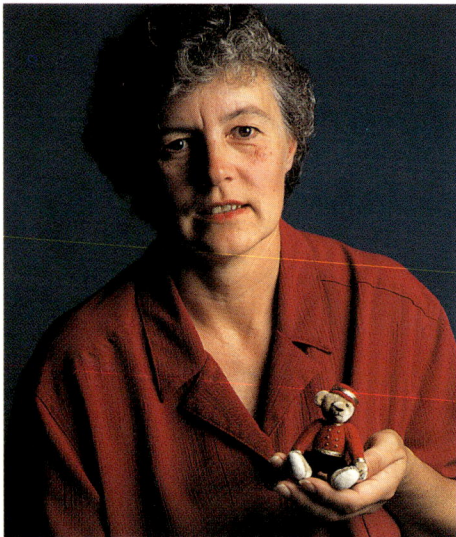

Sylvana with one of her little bell-hop bears.

A friend talked Sylvana into taking her mini bears and toys to a doll show in 1983, where she immediately sold out and was besieged with requests for more. Although she now concentrates on bears, Sylvana still accessorises many of them with tiny toys, embroidered clothes, quilts and pillows.

With her daughter Kimberley's help, she makes between 400 and 600 tiny bears a year, an astonishing output considering all her bears are entirely hand-stitched. Sylvana also spends many hours searching for the right materials. She recently found a perfect tiny yellow check for an edition of Rupert Bears. Sylvana sells her bears at the five to seven shows she attends each year, and fans of her work know to be quick as she always sells out early. Her work has appeared in both Australian and American bear magazines.

'I never imagined that the first tiny bear I made so long ago would have made such a big change in my life. Thanks to that tiny bear, I now have a wonderful hobby and business. The greatest pleasure I get from this is to see a smile on a collector's face when they look at my bears.'

Raggedy bear girl with raggedy ann doll, 10 cm (4") and 3.5 cm (1⅜"), made in 1990.

Teddy bear picnic, from 1992, with bears around 2.5 cm (1") tall on a base 7 cm (2¾") square. The tiniest picnic Sylvana has ever made.

18

CINDY McDONALD

Jumbuck Bears Pty Ltd

*H*AVING DECIDED TO retreat from the hectic pace of city life and move to the country, I found myself contemplating the future one day. During a deep and meaningful conversation with Ted (my trusty childhood bear) we came up with the idea of making teddy bears. I think it was more Ted's idea than mine. He had visions of being surrounded by furry friends and I didn't have the heart to tell him that his Mum couldn't sew! After

a few surprisingly less than disastrous attempts, I was on my way."

Cindy made her first bear in July 1993, and by early 1994 was selling her work through local shops and advertising in bear magazines. She is one of the few artists not to have a craft or arts background, and even her mother was surprised when she started making bears, saying 'But Cindy, you can't sew!'. Her husband, Derek, is a firm believer in her work, and shares the workload of designing, jointing and stuffing.

Cindy and Derek work full-time at their teddy-bear supply business (Beary Cheap Bear Supplies), so they only manage to make around 25 bears a year. Jumbuck Bears are usually limited editions of five or one-offs, as Cindy finds this gives her more time to experiment with designs and fabrics. She believes that with bear-making the face makes the bear, and that matching fabrics to patterns can make all the difference. She sees her work as becoming more and more adventurous over time as she strives to create a different bear that has that special 'something'. Her favourite size to make are the big bears of 60 cm (24") and over.

Jumbuck Bears are sold retail at shows and wholesale to shops around Australia. They can be identified by a small hand-

Pedro, 35 cm (14"), in English crushed mohair with calfskin pawpads, glass eyes and floppy poly/pellet stuffing. A limited edition of five.

written leather tag in the middle of their back seam, which Cindy likes as it is 'unobtrusive and uncommercial'.

Cindy's bears 'Torvil and Dean' received the highest auction bid at the International Bear Fair, held at Darling Harbour in September 1994, and her work has appeared in several newspapers and Australian bear magazines. 'I think my greatest achievement to date, however, is turning my bear-making hobby into a successful bear-making supply business, which keeps me in constant contact with other bear-makers.' Cindy and Derek currently attend six to eight shows a year around the country.

Cindy especially likes the fact that her bears will hopefully become lifelong companions to their owners:

'I once sold a bear to a lady called Frankie who was buying it for a friend visiting from America. This friend was an avid bear collector and was reported to have over 4000 bears in his basement! Frankie found that she could not part with the bear she had chosen for him, so she bought him another. This bear also became part of her family and so another Jumbuck Bear was purchased for her friend. And what do you know, she couldn't part with this one either! I don't know if her friend finally went home with one of our bears; if not, Frankie's house sports a fine collection of Jumbuck Bears.'

Cindy with Bartholemew, 79 cm (31"), in curly English mohair, a limited edition of five.

Bartholemew and Sebastian (back row), both 79 cm (31"); with Pedro and Logan (middle row), 40 cm (16"), in loganberry mohair; and Hartley and Tash (front row, 25 cm (10") and 23 cm (9"). Hartley, Logan and Tash are open editions.

Some of Collette's bears, in mohair.

COLLETTE MITREGA

Bow Bears Pty Ltd

WHILE COLLETTE HAS always had a love of fabrics and toys, she confesses she never really put the two together to create anything worth keeping, until she was inspired by a visit to Ian Pout's bear shop in Witney, England. Then she came across the American bear magazines and, having discovered the world of bears, sent off for a pattern and supplies – and away she went.

Collette made her first bear in 1986 but only started selling her work in 1992, as her work commitments (as a human resources manager) and a young son only allow her to make bears part-time. Even

so, she makes around 50 bears a year, working alone and mostly creating one-offs in her favourite size range of 30 cm (12") to 40 cm (16"). Bow Bears have a label with green lettering in the back seams, and all are in mohair. Collette has not entered her work in competitions and does not advertise, but sells through shows and shops.

Collette finds bear-making very relaxing and therapeutic, especially after a stressful day at the office, and gets a great deal of satisfaction in selling her bears to bear lovers. In the future she would like to combine bear-making and raising her family without the stress of office work. Collette says that bears 'have a magic of their own and when you are working magic, nothing can go wrong !'.

Collette with her bears.

GLORIA MORLEY

Belly-Button Bears

Always a devotee of arts and crafts, Gloria was a graphic artist for a large retail chain when a bear changed her life. She fell in love with and purchased a large green bear named Paddy, and he made her attempt to make a friend for him.

This was only in 1994, and in less than a year Gloria has made Paddy over 80 furry friends. She was surprised and delighted to find that, after exhibiting at only two shows, some of her bears were selected by a leading supplier and a collector to be displayed in exhibitions in Germany and Japan, where they were very well received.

Her Belly-Button Bears are all identified by a bright gold button in their bellies, although Gloria finds that her inspiration comes from many different themes and her bears have many different looks.

Gloria has won prizes for her bears and thoroughly enjoys her newfound career. She thinks that one of the best aspects of it is the opportunity to meet fascinating people and to make new friends.

Gloria with Timothy, 46 cm (18"), in espresso-coloured hand-dyed mohair with ultrasuede paws, glass eyes and check trousers with braces and brown shoes; and Matilda, 56 cm (22"), in old gold English mohair with suede paws, glass eyes, and spoon and apron made from an original Australian flourbag. Both poly/pellet-filled and limited editions.

Group of Gloria's bears (clockwise from left): Billy the Kid, 37 cm (14½"), in mohair with blue hat; Jefferson, 56 cm (22"), in hand-dyed cotton with feathered headband and waistcoat; Angelique, 26 cm (10¼") in cinnamon rayon with flower halo and wings; Oliver, 61 cm (24"), in mohair with country print jacket; Pavlova, 53 cm (21"), in mohair with country-print tutu; Zachary, 52 cm (20½"), in mohair with waistcoat, bow tie and glasses; and Prudence in rose mohair with a strawberry pincushion and a tape-measure tail. All limited editions.

ELAINE PEARCE

Sheltens Original Bears

ALTHOUGH ELAINE made her first bear 15 years ago, it wasn't until three years ago that she attempted her second. Encouraged by her family, she began to sell her bears through shows and shops, and bear-making for her is now a full-time business. With a background in selling and teaching crafts, as well as part-time dressmaking, Elaine sees bear-making as a continuation of her craft career.

She always works alone on her one-off bears, but her limited editions receive the added attentions of her daughter Kristina. Working as many as 12 hours a day, six days a week, Elaine makes about 150 bears a year. She works on the bears' characters and finds that these change over time as she refines her designs. Although she has made miniatures, Elaine prefers to work within the 40 cm (16") to 60 cm (24") size range. Sheltons Original Bears have a sewn-in label giving their catalogue number and date of birth, and all are signed. Elaine sells both wholesale and retail, and also

Elaine with Gizmo, 44 cm (17¼"), in tan mohair, and Becky, 40 cm (16"), in gold mohair. Both bears are poly/pellet-filled.

(Right) Amy, 42 cm (16½"), a one-off bear with poly/pellet stuffing.

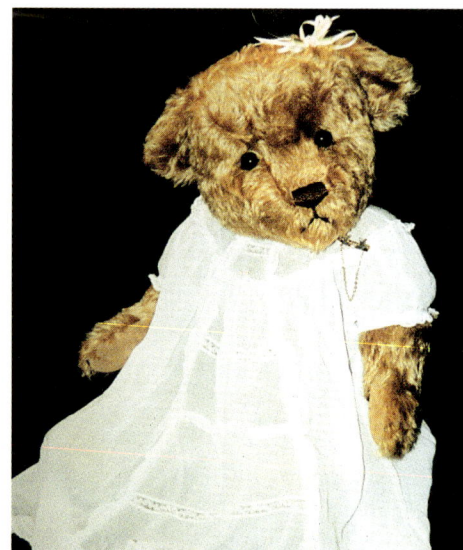

attends about four shows a year.

Elaine's bears have appeared in local papers as well as in Australian bear magazines, but she thinks that her best achievement so far is in selling every bear she has made, most before they are finished.

Smoky, 75 cm (30"), in hand-stressed mohair with cloth pawpads, a growler and poly/pellet filling.

SUSAN PRIEST

Paw Relations

S USAN MADE HER first bear in 1993 after discovering a book in the library on bear-making. She experimented and produced a cute but rather fat and floppy bear. It led her to search for more bear-making information, and it also marked the beginning of her bear-making career. After the bear she had made for a friend's baby was spotted, she received her first commission. Even now, Susan finds most of her orders come by referral and she only has time for retail sales. Susan has always enjoyed artwork and handicrafts in her spare time, but now finds that she has little time for anything but bear-making.

Both hand-stitching and working alone on her bears are very important to Susan. 'Hand-stitching and constructing the bears personally gives them their own individuality. I feel that if someone else helped me to make them, they wouldn't be my bears.' Susan makes only around 15 of her special bears each

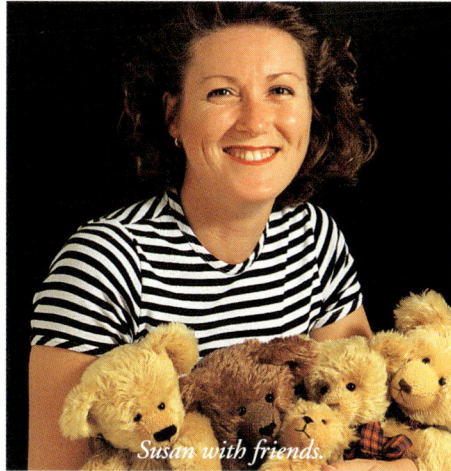
Susan with friends.

year, but this is mainly because she has a full-time career as a flight attendant that involves long trips away from home. Her work also means that some of her bears are very well travelled, and are occasionally delivered to their owners personally. She is especially pleased that one of her bears is now on permanent display in the Teddy Bear Museum of Naples, Florida.

Many Paw Relations bears are one-offs, as Susan likes to experiment with different designs. When she develops a bear that really appeals, it becomes part of an open edition, and Susan intends to create some limited editions in the future.

She likes working with 38 cm (15") and smaller sizes, as her insistence on hand-stitching means that making bears of a larger size is very time consuming. In keeping with the Paw Relations logo, Susan's bears have a small leather patch sewn onto their bottoms. They also have a Paw Relations woven tag in the closing seam in their backs.

Susan believes that the ideal bear should be not only cute enough to catch the eye, but strong enough to fulfil the ultimate role of any Ted as a childhood companion. Her bears fulfil both these criteria.

In spite of 'sore fingers and fur all over the house', for Susan bear-making is worthwhile. She loves to see each bear's personality reveal itself, as a few pieces of fur fabric and stuffing metamorphose into a little character.

At present Susan is changing her hours of work to enable her to devote more time and energy to her bear-making. She hopes that in the future she can open a shop with her husband, Gwyn, incorporating his artistic skills with her own.

'In a time of mass-produced items, I think it is wonderful to be able to obtain a product that is individual and special. Each of my bears incorporates good design, workmanship and care, and every stitch is hand-worked to last a lifetime.'

Bevan, 38 cm (15"), an early one-off from 1994 in swirly gold mohair with suede pawpads; Briar, 43 cm (17"), an open-edition bear in tipped mohair with suede pawpads, glass eyes and a growler; and Bowen, 40 cm (16"), in brown swirly mohair with suede pawpads, glass eyes and poly/pellet filling.

Gwyn, 33 cm (13"), a one-off in swirly gold mohair with suede pawpads, glass eyes and poly/pellet filling.

GLENYS RAMAGE

Down to the Woods

GLENYS STILL HAS her childhood bear, one of a family made for her by her mother. A high-school music teacher for many years, Glenys has always been involved in various arts and crafts and became interested in teddies while learning about porcelain doll-making. In 1990 she made her first bear in synthetic fabric, and is pleased to have won a first ribbon in her first competition but it was not until she left teaching in 1993 that teddies became a way of life for Glenys.

Craft-market sales led to the doll and bear show circuits, which, combined with advertising and mail order, tend to be Glenys's main outlets. As an experienced teacher she enjoys passing on skills and knowledge, so she now also teaches bear-making.

Although her husband makes the joints, Glenys does all the work herself and hand-stitches all her bears. They range from 8 cm (3½") to 46 cm (18"), and Glenys especially enjoys making the small bears. She works with unusual fabrics as well as mohair, currently favouring cotton and a woollen fur, and delights in the wonderful array of materials now available. She is also experimenting with vegetable dyes.

Glenys with friends.

Miniature bears in upholstery velvet, all fully jointed and from 7 cm (2¾") to 8 cm (3½") tall.

Mitch and Buster, 25 cm (10") and Clara 35 cm (14"), in antique-like wool and hand-stitched.

ROMY ROEDER

Vagabond Bears, by Romy

A NEWCOMER TO THE bear-artist world, Romy has for over 20 years been one of Australia's top antique bear and toy authorities, and possibly the first antiques dealer in the country to specialise in bears, dolls and toys. In July 1994 her friend Jenny Laing finally convinced her that old bears were not the only bears, and Romy began to create her own style of bear. Within a few months she started to sell her bears, first at the Sydney International Bear Fair in September 1994, where her bears quickly found homes around the country. Now Romy is selling them around the world and her natural artistic flair is finding a terrific outlet.

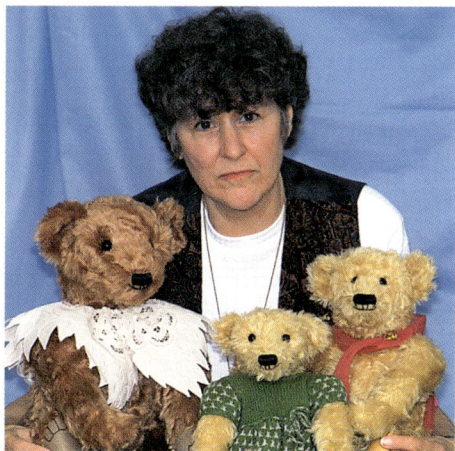

Romy with friends.

Yet to determine her annual production, Romy makes a couple of bears a week and does all the work alone. She says that she works full-time on creating her bears, 'apart from writing and researching articles for various publications and doing all her own photography!' Romy is pleased that after her success in the area of antique bears and toys she is now doing so well with creating her own bears.

Without really trying, Romy says, her bears turn out the way she likes them, cheeky and a little on the scruffy

Otto the Bell-hop, 48 cm (19"), in hand-dyed mohair. Partly hand-sewn and a one-off.

side. Romy makes her bears to be descendants of her very old bears, often using sparse mohair to capture that pre-loved look. They certainly inherit lots of that old-bear charm. Romy's bears are lovable creatures, her ideal bear being one that looks at you pleading to be picked up and hugged. Latest in the line of Romy's bears are a series of wonderful yes/no bears. Waiting for the end result is what Romy enjoys most in making each bear, and her advice to other bear-makers is: always do your own thing!

An unusual stocky and short-limbed old bear, who Romy bought recently at a collectables fair, has made quite an impression on Romy's bear-making. His origins were finally traced in an article by Gerry Grey in the English magazine *Teddy Bear Times*. He was made around 1930 as Winnie the Pooh by the early English bear manufacturers The Teddy Toy Co. Romy was so taken with her rare early Pooh bear that she felt compelled to design a pattern after him, and her 'young Winnies' (available in two sizes) are proving popular.

Romy's bears are one-offs, limited editions and open editions, and she enjoys making a range of sizes from 29 cm (11½") to about 56 cm (22"), which she sells both retail and wholesale. Her bears are partly machine-sewn and partly

hand-sewn. Vagabond Bears can be identified by a cloth label sewn into the back seam, and also by an attached cardboard tag.

Romy's work has appeared in many Australian, English, German and American publications, and besides writing articles for them she has also written four books on collecting dolls and toys, one book on teddy bears and golliwogs (still available) and another that appeared in 24 monthly instalments in *Carter's Antiques & Collectables* magazine.

Two versions of Master Clown, 43 cm (17"), in hand-dyed mohair with felt pawpads, brown glass eyes, red nose and mouth, and claw stitching. Partly hand-sewn and an open edition, 1994.

The Jelly Bean Cubs, 38 cm (15"), in hand-dyed mohair with felt pawpads and brown glass eyes. Partly hand-sewn. Each comes with its own little box of jelly beans.

JENNY ROUND

Round-a-bout Bears

JENNY ORIGINALLY started as a collector, but in 1987, with encouragement from her husband, she decided to try making a bear from a magazine pattern. From the start she was determined to perfect the result and within eight months was pleased enough with her work to begin selling it.

Bear-making now occupies all her time and, although her daughter sometimes assists with the cutting out, all Jenny's work and designs are her own. She produces around 300 bears a year and sells both retail and wholesale, attending about eight shows each year all around Australia.

Jenny has a background in fine arts, having spent three years at college studying ceramics. Since turning to bear-making she has received many first prizes at shows around the country, appeared in many books and publications and also has her bears featured in a range of gift cards by photographer Neill Bartlett. One of the most interesting developments with her bears is her involvement with the 'Make a Wish' Foundation. Bertram, her celebrity bear, was photographed with a large number of local and overseas celebrities for this charity venture.

Jenny makes bears from 7.5 cm (3") to 60 cm (24"), presenting her customers with a large range of sizes and styles from which to choose. Her bears are identified by a cloth tag carrying her logo, along with a card detailing their name and materials used. Her styles are constantly changing as she searches for something different, so all her edition sizes are limited. She thinks that making the ideal bear would be impossible as it would mean the end of creativity, and hopes that her creations will be known for their quality, character and original design.

Jenny finds her biggest frustration lies in the limited range of materials available, but the enjoyment she finds in sculpting the bears' faces and seeing their characters come to life more than compensates for this. Her advice to the budding bear artist is: persevere!

Jenny's bear-making has taken her on several overseas trips and many of her bears go to American collectors, so she is fast establishing her international reputation. It is not hard to see why her original creations have attracted such interest.

A 40 cm (16") open-edition bear in swirly mohair and striped waistcoat, with Thomas (in the billycart), 42 cm (17"), in sparse mohair, and a limited edition of 25.

Jenny with close friend Forrester, 61 cm (24"), a centre-seam mohair bear. Limited edition of 50.

Left to right: a 47 cm (19"), centre-seam mohair, open-edition bear; Elspeth, 43 cm (17"), in mohair wearing a hand-knitted and 'aged' cardigan; and a little 2.5 cm (1") sparse mohair, open-edition bear in striped rompers.

Jennifer with Benson, 66 cm (26"), a one-of-a-kind bear in gold mohair with leather pawpads.

JENNIFER SHAW

Lairdswood Bears

Wesley, Bailey (sitting) and baby Joel, ranging from 23 cm (9") to 56 cm (22"), in gold mohair with leather pawpads and glass eyes or bootbutton eyes (Joel).

C OMING FROM AN artistic family, Jennifer has tried her hand at many crafts, including découpage and pottery, and she has always been expert at sewing. Her interest in bears began about six years ago when she attended a patchwork bear class and was subsequently besieged with bear requests from her 13 nieces and nephews. She filled their orders for ballet bears, fireman bears, army, cowboy and Star Wars bears, and found she was sold on bear-making. She decided to take a few more classes from some of the recognised bear artists, and this in turn led to the discovery of mohair and other supplies. As her skills improved she enquired about promoting her bears and organising the use of the Australian Made accreditation.

Jennifer makes all her bears herself and feels they would lose their originality if she were to employ others. She makes over 60 a year and supplies a number of

Millie, 61 cm (24"), in long wavy mohair with brown glass eyes.

shops in her area. Her bears are mostly one-of-a kinds, although she has just completed a limited edition of Zodiac Bears, as well as a pair of dressed bears for a debutante ball. Lairdswood Bears have a small tag sewn into the back seam and all carry the Australian Made symbol.

During the last bushfires in NSW one of my bears, a little fellow called Smoky, accompanied the fire crew during the firefighting and co-ordinating efforts. He was rewarded for his help, invited to a presentation dinner afterwards and had his photo taken by a Newcastle newspaper!

KAREN STEWART

Wern Danstey Farm Bears

KAREN HAD LONG felt a need to make her own bear having never had a proper teddy as a child, and she finally persuaded her friend Jennifer Laing to teach her in 1991. It was the first bear-making class that Jennifer had ever taught, so both of them were learning together. With a background in handicrafts and embroidery, Karen quickly took to her new hobby and in the same year started selling her bears, both wholesale and retail. As she has a full-time career elsewhere, she only works at her bears in her spare time, making around 30 a year.

Karen has won many prizes for her bears and is pleased at the recognition they are gaining. Most of her bears are one-offs or small editions of five and 10, and her preferred sizes range from 20 cm (8") to 30 cm (12"). All her bears are traditional in style, made in mohair and entirely hand-stitched. They have a small leather identification label in their lower back seam. Karen likes to make bears in unusual colours and insists on using the best materials available.

Karen's bears are very adventurous. One has sailed with Don McIntyre to Antarctica to raise money for the Royal Alexandra Hospital for Children, and another has yet to return from an attempt to climb Mt Makalu in the Himalayas!

(Above) My Bear, 38 cm (15"), a one-off in sparse German mohair and filled with coconut fibre.

(Left) BD. Bear, 48 cm (19"), in German mohair with leather pawpads and glass eyes. Bear of Show at Brisbane's Winter Wonderland show in 1993.

Karen at work.

Jasper, Patrick and Gus, 17 cm (6¾") to 23 cm (9"), in German mohair. Limited editions of 10 each.

PAT TOMLINSON

Oz-Born Bears

*P*AT IS ONE OF Australia's 'first generation' of bear artists, who started making bears around 1980. Originally from England, where she studied at the College of Arts in Blackpool, Pat made her first bear when a student asked her to design one for her.

Bear-making is not a full-time occupation for Pat, who also deals in antiques, and her output is limited as she does all the work herself. She mostly sells retail, and has made bears in all sizes, from 2.5 cm (1") to 1.5 m (5 ft) high. Her bears are mostly one-offs or very small editions. Pat is known for using a variety of antique fur fabrics in natural tones to great effect. She says that her bears 'look as if they have just hidden the honey and aren't telling you where it is'. Oz-Born bears can be identified by a tag on their left-hand side.

Pat's vision of the ideal bear is one that appeals to everybody, and she finds that her bears are changing in style as she discovers new and different fabrics to work with. She works hard on her designs and her quality workmanship shows in each bear. She enjoys 'getting a wink and a nod from each bear to say when he's just right'.

Pat attends five or six shows a year and finds that, apart from the aches and pains associated with sewing, and the initial frustration of supplies being unavailable, bear-making presents a continuing and satisfying challenge. Her advice for anyone starting out is to begin with a medium-sized bear before working up or down.

Pat has won various blue ribbons from shows around Australia, as well as prizes from English shows. Her work has appeared in several notable books, including Linda Mullins's *Teddy Bears Past and Present* and Doris and Terry Michaud's *Contemporary Teddy Bear Price Guide*.

Pat with Ernestine, 46 cm (18"), a prototype in antique white feather mohair, and Scruffy, 15 cm (6"), in plush with guardhairs, a limited edition of 25.

Poopidoo, 30 cm (12"), a prototype in pink mohair with bootbutton eyes; a Sailor Monkey, 38 cm (15"), in plush, felt and velour with safety eyes; and Honey, 23 cm (9"), in plush with guardhairs, leather pawpads and glass eyes.

Kerry II, 80 cm (31½"), in mohair with suede pawpads and glass eyes, designed to sit astride a rocking horse; with Ernestine and Prince of the Park, 40 cm (16"), in mohair and tapestry with bootbutton eyes, leather shoes and a velvet cape.

KAY VANDERLEY

Completely Stuf'd

BACK IN 1985, Kay saw an article on a bear collector in an American doll magazine and, while she couldn't relate to the dolls, thought 'Now teddy bears are something I could get into...' She thought she would collect them, but on a subsequent trip to the United States was dismayed by the prices (and the weak Aussie dollar), so instead she brought home some fur fabric and a book on how to make bears. Entirely self-taught, with no formal arts training, Kay used to make patchwork quilts until the bears took over her sewing machine.

Kay began the long process of defining and creating her personal look, and the style she has established in her bears – long limbs, humps, little beady eyes and impish expressions – is known and loved everywhere. She works alone, which she says sometimes drives her bananas, and tends to make bears part-time, creating 100-150 bears a year. Her first bears sold in a local craft shop/tea-room, but they are now found in the best teddy-bear shops around the country.

Kay's bears are either open editions or editions of 10 or less. As she buys small quantities of different fur with which to experiment, she sometimes cannot reproduce a particular bear as she forgets which fur she used. Her ideal bear is a 1904 Steiff and, as she likes the classic style and natural colours, she avoids gimmicks and distortions. Kay feels that 'the bears should be fairly neutral to allow the owner to use their imagination to "fill in" the bear's character. If I do too much, then I've had all the fun, and leave nothing for the new owner to do.' Her preferred bear size is 40 cm (16"), 'good for hugging and playing with', but finds her smaller 28 cm (11") size is more popular. Her favourite bear is always the last bear she made, as she feels she is improving all the time. Completely Stuf'd bears have a leather stamped tag sewn into the back seam. As of 1995, these tags are also dated.

Kay's least favourite part of bear-making is sewing in paw pads, but the finished bear makes her smile and makes it all worthwhile. Her advice to other bear-makers is: 'Use the best materials and sew them strongly, especially the eyes. Make a bear that will last a hundred years!'.

Kay says of her bears, 'Someone at a fair once looked at my bears and said, "Your bears are witty" – I quite liked that ... Bears of Great Wit'.

Tavish, 40 cm (16"), an open edition, and Toulous, 28 cm (11"), a limited edition of 10.

Kay with an armful of friends.

A group of Completely Stuf'd Bears, from 12 cm (4¾") to 40 cm (16"), all in mohair with leather pawpads and glass eyes.

HELEN WILLIAMS

Bear-Foot Bears

ONE OF THE youngest bear-makers, Helen has just turned 16 and began making bears two years ago when her mother bought her *The Art of Making Teddy Bears.* Her first bear, called Fred, was made from felt, and Helen says that although cute he was rather strange looking. Nonetheless, he was promptly bought by a friend and her bear business took off from there.

After developing her own patterns, Helen approached some bear shops with some of her work and is now supplying them with her bears. As she is still at school, bear-making is a part-time job for her and she averages about 10 bears a year. Helen's favourite size is a medium bear of around 36 cm (14"). Her Bear-Foot bears wear cardboard swing-tags with their details.

Helen sees her bears as remaining traditional in style even as she becomes more skilled. She hopes that her work is distinguished by the care taken in the making of each bear as well as by the appeal of the finished teddy.

Helen with Alexander, Jeremy and Emily, all 35 cm (14"), in German mohair and acrylic. Jeremy is a limited edition, the others are one-offs.

LORIS HANCOCK

Studio Seventy

ALTHOUGH LORIS FIRST played with bears and bear-making as a child, using her dressmaking mother's material scraps, she made her first bear only five years ago for her cousin who was in hospital. It was received with such enthusiasm that Loris now makes her one for every birthday and Christmas.

Involved with arts and crafts since high school, where she designed a range of wooden toys and rag dolls, Loris went on to get diplomas in Ceramics, Interior Design and Creative Food Studies. Her first show was in 1990 at 'Winter Wonderland' in Brisbane, where her rag dolls and beaded bears proved popular.

Loris makes bears full-time and does all her work 'very alone, until late at night, while watching TV with a snoring husband keeping me company!'. She makes around 100 bears a year, in limited editions of five up to 25, and as one-offs. Her favourite size is about 7.5 cm (3"), because she hates stuffing the big bears. Loris attends five or six shows a year and also sells kits to budding bear-makers.

Loris has won several prizes in major shows and has appeared in both national and international bear magazines, but thinks her best achievement to date is winning first prize for Woodland Bear at the First Sydney International Bear Fair . 'This was equal to convincing my husband, Bob, to mind my trading table at the Tropicarnival Doll Show, where he planned a New Zealand Bear Holiday, which I managed to turn into a San Diego Bear Holiday'.

Friends and relatives are often unwitting models for her character bears, but are flattered when they find out that they provide inspiration for her work. This, combined with Loris's renowned use of different colour combinations, fabrics and bead ornamentation, produces truly unique bears. Her bears are individually numbered, signed and dated on a certificate, with a signed tag tied to the leg, and all are individually boxed.

Loris is continually experimenting with her work and finds satisfaction in achieving the individual expressions and characters in her little bears, as well as in the pleasure they bring to people. She hopes that her bears will give her the means to holiday around the world with her secretary/business manager (husband).

Her advice to new bear-makers is: be patient, meticulous and don't talk to strange men at bear shows. The only problem is, she says, there are never enough strange men at bear shows!

Good Luck Charm Bear, 10 cm (4"), in a range of colours, limited edition of 25, each with its own charm and instructions in scroll.

Loris holding Blokie Bear.

Group of Loris's bears (from back left): Warren the Wizard, Fantasy Bear, Scruffy, Debbie, mini Golliwog, Bob E Bear, Baby Bernard (brown), Blokie and Baby Bernard (gold). All in mohair and mini bear fabric, from 7.5 cm (3") to 15 cm (6"), and mostly in limited editions.

Hi Ho Honey Bear, 7.5 cm (3"), a mini cowboy with a wooden honey pot and gold bell on a 11.5 cm (4½") mohair riding bear. A limited edition of five.

JANE HIGGINS

Straw Beary Designs

JANE FIRST DISCOVERED bears eight years ago when roaming museums overseas. While modern-day equivalents did not hold her interest, Jane was fascinated by the ragged museum bears she saw. 'Those qualities that only arise after a century are what I try to capture.' Jane first started selling her bears at Brisbane's South Bank craft markets three years ago, and now also sells to selected shops, as well as through the six or seven shows she attends each year.

In between raising her two children, Jane makes around 300 bears a year, ranging from 10 cm (4'') to 40 cm (16''), and doing all the bear-making herself. Her bears are always dressed, but none of them is dressed exactly the same, even if they belong to the same era. 'Recently, I have found an interesting theme in the US Civil War because of the variety of the uniforms worn by the soldiers. Their shoes wore out, their coats burned and they were dirtied. They were all heroes.' Jane's other lines include sailor bears and lace doily bears. They have an identifying label sewn into their clothes and her larger bears usually have a tag in the left ear depicting a red 'Straw Beary' on a white background.

Jane has appeared in various craft and home-decorating magazines as well as newspapers. Because her mother (who makes porcelain dolls) and her sister (who makes golliwogs) also attend various shows with her, articles are often written about the three of them.

Jane Higgins

Civil War bears, 20 cm (8''), in German mohair. They have been aged through staining and stitching and have 'powder' burns in their clothes.

Larger bear, 28 cm (11"), in English mohair with suede pawpads and glass eyes.

June with her childhood bear.

JUNE KITTLETY

Bear Fantastique

JUNE STARTED MAKING bears seven years ago after reading an article in the American magazine *Teddy Bear and Friends*. Little did she know at the time that it would lead to a career, and that she would make over 2000 bears (to date) who would have homes all over the world.

Teddies have always been important to June and she still has her own, which was given to her on her fourth birthday. Bears seem to be important in her family's life too. When her daughter was married, June made not only the clothes for the bridal party, but also the attendants' gifts (of bears dressed to match them), which served as table decorations.

When June was first designing her patterns she had a 'dudley bucket' (for the duds that didn't quite measure up), which was always a popular playing spot with visiting children. The first 30 cm (12") pattern has now developed into around 20 different designs, with sizes ranging from 7.5 cm (3") to 46 cm (18") and in fabrics that include mohair, cashmere, alpaca and acrylics. June does all the work herself, including making the wooden discs she uses as joints. Her bears have a swing tag, whose logo is a sepia photo of June's mother as a child with her little bear. She has a selection of limited editions as well as a standard range, and sells through stores around the country and at shows.

The show circuit has come full circle, and June now judges at some venues.

Miniatures from 7.5 cm (3") to 10 cm (4"), in acrylic with glass eyes and handmade outfits.

JUDI NEWMAN

Art Bears

Judi in her workshop.

BEARS HAVE LONG provided Judi with security. On leaving her country home at 17 to attend a city university, she took her husband's childhood Ted with her. Later, as a bear collector, she discovered that even in Europe old bears were very expensive and the modern plush bears didn't appeal to her. After returning home from her European tour in 1990 Judi designed her first antique reproduction bear. In 1991, when a friend took five of her bears to a large Melbourne bear shop and they ordered 26, Judi found herself in business.

At the moment Judi is a schoolteacher, as well as teaching bear-making classes, but one day she hopes to make bears her full-time career. She draws on the expertise of several bear-making helpers when needed, as well as a secretarial service. She makes around 100 open edition and limited edition bears in mohair each year, and another 500 bear kits and projects. Her favourite size is 30 cm (12") and her favourite style is her new 'Worn and Torn' series. Judi's bears sell both wholesale and retail, and she attends several shows a year.

Art Bears have a woven label on their left foot and a swing tag with a gold charm, and can also be identified by their distressed or aged mohair, short rounded limbs, shaved noses, and black eyes and noses.

Judi advises people to join the bear world. 'It's great fun and a serious addiction. Many bear people are very helpful and caring, they are also very professional and dedicated. It may seem at first a frivolous business but this is far from the truth.'

A cuddle of Art Bears, from 30 cm (12") to 50 cm (20").-

Judi's Worn and Torn series, all 30 cm (12"), with her old bears in the middle at the rear and lower right. Tori (left), a one-off; Edwina (front), a cover bear from Australian Country Craft *magazine; and Stringbear (right), a very popular feather-soft bear.*

LYN WILSON

Lyn's Tiny Corners

MAKING STUFFED TOYS in hospital before the birth of her first child led Lyn to making bears. An interest in miniatures resulted in her first tiny bear, made in felt in 1981. In 1982 her first customer bought her little bears as accessories for her porcelain baby dolls, and Lyn finds that even today many notable doll artists enhance their dolls with her bears.

Working alone, Lyn produces up to 2000 of her tiny teddies each year, an incredible ouput. A small tag around each bear's neck gives its details. Most of them are open editions with a few one-offs and limited editions, and Lyn likes them small. 'The tinier, the better!' Her aim is to produce the smallest achievable fully jointed fur bear.

She has won several awards in Queensland and in Canada, has had reviews of her work in Australian bear magazines and is also a feature writer on bears. Lyn sees herself as 'a quiet achiever with a commitment to producing quality miniature bears'.

Mollie Beartrix (front), 5.5 cm (2¼"), and Cranston John (rear), 7.5 cm (3"). Both bears have jointed limbs but fixed heads in the Australian Joy Toy Bears tradition.

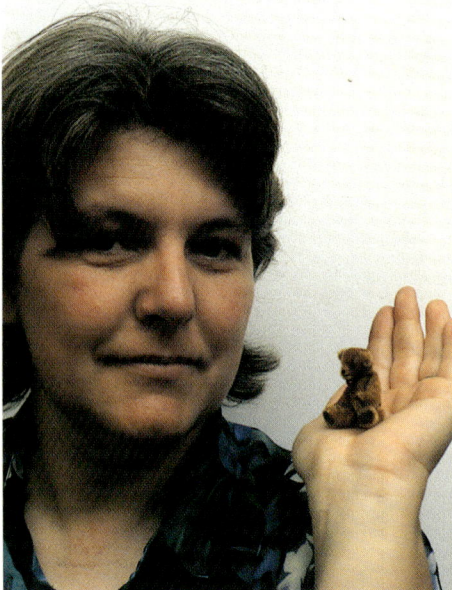

Lyn Wilson

Freddie, 4 cm (1¼"), fully jointed, in soft synthetic fur with leather footpads and felt rompers.

36

Tiger Kelly, 56 cm (22"), in German mohair with glass eyes.

Jean-Luc, 50 cm (20"), in German mohair with ultrasuede pawpads and glass eyes.

Monty, 56 cm (22"), in German V-cut mohair with glass eyes.

MARLENE DE LORENZO

Grubby Bears

MARLENE HAS BEEN fostering bears for as long as she can remember, her first bear having been bought for her by her grandmother on the day she was born. A traumatic experience involving her favourite filthy bear being washed and 'killed' made her vow that her bears would never be cleaned again, and 'Marlene's grubby bears' became a catchphrase. Many years later it seemed only appropriate that it should also be the name of Marlene's handmade bears.

Marlene first began making bears about five years ago, when she was feeling low and remembered what comfort and support her Big Ted had provided. She thought that everyone should be given the excuse to have a Big Ted, and so her first bears were made as gifts.

A degree in Visual and Performing Arts helped Marlene with the visualising and creating of these lovable works of art, and she now finds it

Marlene with Ginger, 52 cm (20½"), in swirly mohair with glass eyes.

difficult to keep up with the demand for her bears. She has given up her job as arts consultant for the Victorian Education Department and now works full-time on her bears, and also finds the time to teach bear-making classes. Finding it difficult to buy good materials, Marlene established a bear supply company called Teddy's Bits Pty Ltd, and imports large quantities of mohair from Germany as well as

acrylics from France and Korea. Australian companies are now producing some very fine plush fabrics and these are included in her range.

Marlene's bears are usually one-offs or very limited editions, as she finds it tedious to reproduce the same thing more than three times. She has yet to develop any particular style, as she says that she does not want her bears to look as though they are all related. She believes that facial expression and posture should be able to express a bear's character fully.

'I enjoy basing my bears on some of the people I have met or read about. I have just created the first of a series of bears based on Bancks's 'Ginger Meggs' series. The town bully, Tiger Kelly, has been created complete with intimidating stance and black eye. To follow will be: Bennie Hooper, Coogan, Jug Ears, Minnie and, of course, Ginger himself. In these characters, Bancks was able to capture the essence of so many individuals we meet in everyday life. I hope my bears might do the same.'

SAMANTHA FREDERICKS

Bliss Toys

SAMANTHA STARTED Bliss Toys in 1993 in the midst of a marketing career, and with an eclectic background in science, fine arts and German. She has just recently given up marketing to follow her heart and develop her own business further. Samantha has always loved and made bears and toys, and 'when my favourite furry friend hurled himself into a raging river after 25 years of valuable service and ran away to start a feral bear colony in the Victorian mountains, I vowed to make thousands in his likeness so that his memory would live on'.

Samantha now works full-time designing and producing 350-400 bears and animals a year, employing four other members of her family part-time in the business. She chose the name 'Bliss' to denote happiness and joy, and 'Toys' to encompass her range of bears and other animals that are both collectable and childsafe. Bliss Toys have found their way to homes around the world and are distributed through a network of retail outlets around Australia and overseas. Two Australian stores carry an exclusive limited-edition bear with a special tag and signed certificate.

Bliss Toys first launched a range of seven limited-edition bears, joined a few months later by several more limited editions. These early editions are now selling out and in June 1994 five more bears joined the Bliss Toys family. Once again limited editions, three of these bears feature hand-dyed mohair coats in exciting green, blue and purple. These vibrant bears have already proved extremely popular.

Each bear in the Bliss Toys family is fully jointed, has an individually numbered tag sewn under its left arm and a Bliss Toys logo on its right foot or back, depending on the size of the bear. Bears range in height from 18 cm (7'') to 43 cm (17'') and come in limited editions of 50–200. All are cotton-stuffed, made in mohair and conform to the Australian Standard for Safety in children's toys.

At the small number of shows Samantha attends each year she launches her one-offs and open edition bears in addition to her current range. These bears and animals of unusual shapes, fabrics and accessories are not necessarily childsafe and are aimed specifically at collectors.

Samantha's favourite aspects of bear-making are developing new patterns and watching them come to life as each step is completed. 'My ultimate goal is for Bliss Toys to be recognised both in Australia and around the world as a proudly Australian producer of fine-quality toys and collectables for children and adults of all ages.'

Mitch, 43 cm (17''), in Alfonzo red mohair with a two-tone nose; and Carl, 34 cm (13½''), a tall, skinny, sparse mohair bear with a waxed nose and pottery bead necklace.

Percy the Lion, 20 cm (8''), a childsafe bear in four different mohairs, with cotton stuffing; Layne, 43 cm (17''), a centre-seam bear in sparse mohair with stencilled pawpads; and Stone, 20 cm (8''), a childsafe bear in gold mohair with a shaved snout.

Samantha and some of her Bliss Toys.

Buddy the polar bear, 46 cm (18''), with leather claws and shoebutton eyes; and penguin friends Clint, 20 cm (8''), and Quinn, 29 cm (11½''), with jointed necks and ultrasuede feet.

Nicole, 50 cm (20"), a traditional-style bear in gold mohair, a limited edition of 30.

A selection of Buzzbee Bears from 7.5 cm (3") to 61 cm (24").

HELEN GODFREY

Buzzbee Bears

HELEN HAS ALWAYS been a bear lover, and it seems to run in the family. Even her mother still has the bear she was given as a child. Helen started experimenting with bear-making in 1984, but was frustrated by the lack of patterns and supplies at that time. She has been selling her work since 1985 and, even though she also has a full-time job, finds that she is planning new designs and ideas at all hours of the day.

Buzzbee Bears are available both wholesale and retail, and are a mix of limited editions and open editions with some made-to-order concepts. Helen finds that she is enjoying making smaller and smaller bears these days, with most being less than 25 cm (10") and many down to 13 cm (5"). Buzzbee Bears have an identification tag sewn into them as well as a swing tag. Most, but not all, have names.

Helen Godfrey, a limited edition of one!

'People tell me they can always pick a Buzzbee Bear, I'm not sure how. Although I do try to make bears that look at you, I think they should still look like animals, not toys. I have fairly conservative tastes in bears and I like them to be a little on the chubby side too. I don't like bears with too many gimmicks on them.'

Helen and her bears have appeared in several national bear magazines and can also be found at the three or four shows she attends each year. Helen's advice to beginners is:

'Use only good-quality materials, experiment with other people's patterns intially or go to a class. Then think for yourself, and remember that a bear is more than a toy. If you're not sure how the bear really looks, hold it up in fornt of a mirror. It is surprising what distortions and mistakes this can show up.'

Ronwyn with Lulu, in swirly German mohair with bootbutton eyes and pinafore dress.

Me and My Little Sister, 18 cm (7"), and 13 cm (5"), in mohair with armature in their arms, wearing matching dresses and holding their teddy and pussycat.

Me and My Pony, 17.5 cm (7"), in distressed German mohair with armature in his arms and handcrafted pony on wheels.

RONWYN GRAHAM

Bambini Design

INSPIRED TO START making bears after learning about artist bears in a magazine, Ronwyn made her first bear in early 1992 and within a few months was selling her work at shows. Ronwyn loved to draw and paint as a child, studied Chinese brush painting for three years and made award-winning porcelain dolls for almost seven years before discovering bears.

Ronwyn works alone, her only help coming from her mother who occasionally assists in pattern-cutting. Making 80-90 bears in the last year, Ronwyn has taken on bear-making as a full-time occupation. She is known for both her miniature bears and her range of mohair bears. Her miniatures are mostly in editions of 15, and even the open editions are numbered and rarely exceed 15-20. While Ronwyn enjoys making the miniatures, she finds that at present she is having more fun with her range of 18 cm (7") bears. Bambini Design bears can be identified by a satin printed ribbon sewn into the centre-back seam

and a printed swing tag. They are sold directly to the collector.

Bambini Design bears have received several awards, as well as a prestigious American TOBY nomination in 1993 and again in 1995, of which Ronwyn is particularly proud. Her work has been featured in several national and international bear magazines and her bears are found in collectors' homes around the world.

'I'm continually creating new designs as part of my evolvement as a bearmaker. An ideal bear for me is any that provokes certain emotion in my heart and says "Here is a living fantasy that actually speaks to me". My recent designs

have changed in their size and fabric. I want to create a childlike innocent look.'

Her tip is: 'Be gentle with yourself. Bear-making can be addictive and many bear-makers expect too much too soon.'

Ronwyn has received many lovely letters and photos of her bears in their new homes. One bear in particular accompanied her new owners to a luxury hotel to celebrate their Christmas and wedding anniversary. Two delightful photos were taken of the bear preparing for a bubble bath and playing with an old-world sailboat. For Ronwyn, this sort of feedback from happy collectors is one of the most enjoyable aspects of bear-making.

Group of Me and My Pony, Me and My Teddy, Little Sister, and Me and My Friends – the TOBY Award nomination for 1995.

SONYA HERON

Heartfelt Bears

*S*ONYA HAS BEEN a bear-maker since she was 12 years old, when her sewing teacher arranged for her bears to be sold through a babywear shop, although she was much more interested in horses. When she finally owned one, her bear-making took a back seat — until she discovered the world of collectable artist bears 18 months ago. She was especially inspired by miniatures and antique-looking bears, and has mastered the art of both. She quickly gained recognition for her fine work and has won first prizes consistently in all her competitions.

Sonya puts her skills at other crafts to good use in her bear-making, which she now does full-time, along with helping to raise a young family. She manages to produce three to six bears a week and supplies several retail outlets. Her favourite bears are the small and very small ones, as she finds them a constant challenge requiring much patience. She is working towards producing the bears she needs for a show circuit as she loves to meet other bear people.

'I love old bears and tend to look for a wistful look in their faces and eyes that indicates wisdom and strength of character. I try to create a little of this in my bears and I love them to look like they have some history or perhaps a story to tell.'

(Right) From Sonya's Loved to Bits range, Frith, 14 cm (5½"), looking after a friend's eggs. Made for an exhibition in a Melbourne Art Gallery, 1994.

New-Old all-fours bear Leroy, 20 cm (8"), in sailor hat and collar with toy ark on wheels; and Cissy, 15 cm (6"), loosely jointed with stitches showing and coconut fibre stuffing spilling out, together with her little 7.5 cm (3") bear toy.

Sonya with her antiqued Jacket Bear, 30 cm (12"), an open edition but each one is different.

Wee Willie Winkie, 30 cm (12"), in night attire and teddy slippers, with his old friend, 14 cm (5½").

CARLENE HUGHES

Honey Pot Bears

'I HAVE BEEN AN avid bear collector for 10 years, and because of my love of small things and because of limited space, I became interested in miniatures. As they were not so plentiful in Australia, I decided to start making my own, but it was my family who encouraged me to start selling them. My professional miniature bear-making career came about quite by accident. I was at a bear shop showing the owner my second miniature when I was told about the Sydney International Bear Fair in 1994. I entered two bears and won first prizes for each, at my first show. That's where it all started.'

Although she has won awards for other crafts, Carlene made her first miniature bear as late as 1994. Soon after Carlene began, her bears became available through several bear shops in Victoria. She has shown amazing skill and versatility for someone just entering the field, and not surprisingly has already won six awards as well as interest from overseas.

Working alone and full-time on her bears, she makes approximately 200 a year. Her little bears have many different characters and are known for their big noses and sweet expressions. Carlene believes that with each new bear her technique is improving and the bears are gaining in general appeal. All her bears come with a name and a swing tag, which is numbered, dated and signed. Their sizes range from 2.5 cm (1") to 10 cm (4") and most are open editions. When Carlene makes a bear she pays meticulous attention to every detail, from the pattern-making, sewing and filling, through to the final touches. A bear must be perfect in her eyes before she will consider selling it.

Carlene's advice to budding bear-makers?

'If you are going to make bears to sell, always try to make something unique. It can be hard sometines. Just as you think of a good idea you can turn around and discover many others have thought of the same thing. But don't give up. If you put effort and love into your bear-making, you will go far.'

Clockwise from left: Suzi, Sugarplum, Blossom, Pip and Twinkle. From 2.5 cm (1") to 7.5 cm (3") and all fully jointed.

Left to right: Frosty the Snow Bear, Mr Watts, Buttons, Podge and Miss Mopsie. From 3 cm (1¼") to 9.5 cm (3¾"). Buttons and Mr Watts were Carlene's first prize-winning bears, in her first competition.

Carlene and an array of her prize-winning Honey Pot Bears.

Clockwise from left: PJ, Robbie with teddy bear, Little Ted, Sam and CB. From 5 cm (2") to 9 cm (3½"), in upholstery fabric, mohair and felt, and all fully jointed.

CHRISTINA JACKSON

Sticky Paws

CHRISTINA HAS ALWAYS had an interest in arts and crafts and is the owner of a small bear collection, but it was not until she took a two-hour bear-making class that she knew she had found her creative niche. She made her first bear ('a very sad-looking creature') in 1989 and first sold professionally in 1992.

Christina has a Floral Art Diploma and continues to operate a florist business specialising in weddings, but she manages to produce many of her bears each year. She has a part-time assistant who helps with the pattern-cutting. Each Sticky Paws bear has a label, along with a Made in Australia label sewn into a seam. The bears range from 7.5 cm (3'') upwards and come in many designs. They sell both wholesale and retail.

Christina's bears have won many prizes and appeared in local newspapers as well as on greeting cards. Christina is delighted with the success of her 'cottage industry' and now cannot imagine a day without bears.

A group of Christina's bears (clockwise from rear left): Annie, Bruno, Brindabella with Bacci (a pair), Chester, Sweet Pea, Rubin and Josh. All in German mohair, from 15 cm (6'') to 50 cm (20'').

Christina with Muffin, 38 cm (15''), in German mohair with glass eyes, cotton/pellet filling and a hand-knitted cardigan; and the Jester, 7.5 cm (3''), sitting on a drum and holding a smaller bear head on a stick. The Jester won a first and Best in Section at the Melbourne Bear Show in 1994.

Dudley, 50 cm (20''), in curly German mohair with glass eyes and poly/pellet filling. A prize-winner at the Regional Bear Show.

POL McCANN

Mitchell Tyrie Bears

POL McCANN (Pol is Gaelic for 'Paul') does not consider himself a bear artist. From the start he aimed to set up a quality Australian bear-manufacturing company, but has probably put more hours into his work and his bears than some solo artists.

He began in 1990, when due to lack of funds he was obliged to make his Christmas gifts. His first bear was a present for his partner, Martin. Mostly self-taught in the bear department, Pol, who is also a creative writer, admits to 'picking the brains of a few friends who are expert sewers'.

Pol put himself in business, and now has a permanent assistant, an office manager and a couple of casual staff members. Even so, Pol works full-time at his bears and for the first three years worked seven days most weeks, often putting in 12–14 hour days. Pol believes that 'an Australian brand can be, and should be, as desirable as an import as long as we strive to maintain quality'. In 1995 Pol is aiming for 1500

Pol Dominic McCann holding Uncle Ted, 70 cm (28"), in curly German mohair with safety eyes, a limited edition of 100 bears per shade; and Little Ivan, 20 cm (8"), in English mohair with safety eyes, a limited edition of 1000.

Gladstone (left), 42 cm (16½"), in German mohair with safety eyes and growler, with his big brother, Evandale, 55 cm (21½"), in similar materials. Part of a three-bear set.

Mitchell Tyrie Bears, and would like that figure to be 4000 by 1998.

Mitchell Tyrie currently has four childsafe bears and 12 limited-edition bears. While he takes the business seriously, Pol writes the catalogues with his tongue firmly in his cheek, and conveys a sense of fun about his bears and their characters. As well as producing the catalogue he runs an extensive advertising campaign each year, and maintains a fairly comprehensive schedule of public appearances around the country and overseas. At the shows he attends he generally offers work that is not available through their retail network, and this allows him some freedom in creative experimentation.

Mitchell Tyrie collectors' bears are named alphabetically and are identified by a white on black label on the bear's left foot, while their childsafe bears wear a white on green label. Pol also uses a white on blue label for workshop bears when he is teaching, which he does through his retail outlets.

Pol and his bears have received a lot of media coverage, but he believes his biggest achievement to date has been in raising over $200,000 for AIDS support

Daniel (standing), 33 cm (13"), in German mohair with safety eyes and growler, available in many colours, with Victor, also 33 cm (13"), an individually 'aged' and numbered bear.

in charity auctions. Every year his bears are dressed by leading Australian and international fashion and theatre houses and are auctioned through Christie's.

'I would like to be employing more people and exporting more, but we have come a long way in four short years, and so far it has just felt like I have been doing my apprenticeship. There is so much to learn, both regarding design and running a business, but I couldn't trade in this life for a nine-to-five again.'

Sterling the Protector, 28 cm (11"), a dragon bear in green mohair with wire-reinforced red French felt wings, tail and paws. A limited edition of 100.

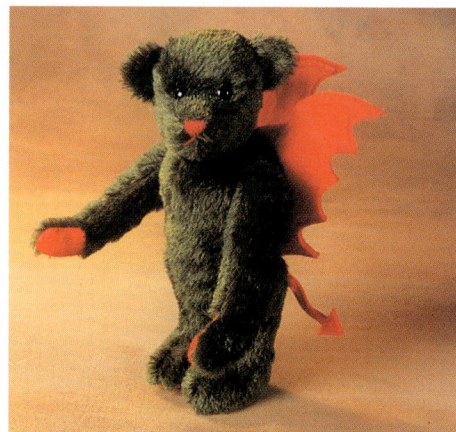

ROSALIE MACLEMAN

Macbears

AN INTEREST IN early character dolls by Steiff, Lenci and Kathy Kruse, and a fascination with textiles, gradually led Rosalie to making toys and eventually to bears. As well as having a background in the arts, having studied graphics and ceramics, Rosalie has been sewing since she was seven, giving her a headstart in the bear-making business. She first started selling her bears in 1991 at craft markets, but quickly graduated to doll and bear shows around Australia.

Rosalie works alone, apart from her husband building the occasional prop for her, and considers herself a mother first and a bear-maker second. Even so, she often puts in over eight hours a day on her bears. Rosalie is known for her outstanding attention to detail and the humour of her designs. She makes only between 30 and 40 bears a year, because each one takes between 50 and 100

hours to make! Not only does she make the character-filled bears, but she also dresses them in hand-smocked outfits, petit-point embroidered pyjamas or dresses, or perhaps in miniature Fair Isle sweaters with handmade leather shoes. Everything is perfect in scale and detail.

Rosalie's bears are mainly limited editions of up to 10, and she makes variations within each edition to stave off the boredom of repeating herself. Her bears are from 40 cm (16") to 50 cm (20") high, as she finds this size range allows her scope to develop a character. Macbears are only sold retail at present. Each bear is identified by the name *Macbears: Rosalie Macleman* on the edge of the right pawpad. A swing tag with the Macbear logo also accompanies the bear.

Although she has entered only a few competitions, Rosalie has won everything she has entered. She says that these wins would be her most easily recognised achievements to date, but she regards her best personal success in bear-making to be the relationships that have developed between her bears and the collectors, many of whom have become her friends.

'It is really nice to be inspired by current bear-makers and their work, but it is ultimately more satisfying and interesting for the maker and the collector if there are new designs emerging. That way bear-making grows and progresses instead of stagnating. So my advice is to strive for quality and originality.'

(Below) Bye Baby Bunting, 35 cm (14"), and Teabag 18 cm (7"). Wool and mohair with a hand-pieced quilt, and embroidered wool drop-tail sleepsuit. Over 50 hours work!

(Centre) Hugh, 40 cm (16"), in camel/mohair with vintage glasses, handmade outfit and hand-knitted cardigan. A limited edtion of 10.

Boomer with his creator, Rosalie. Boomer is 40 cm (16"), in mohair with cotton/wool swimsuit with vintage buttons, matching lifesaver's hat and handmade kangaroo floaty ring. Judged Best Professional Artist Bear at the First Sydney International Bear Fair in 1994.

(Bottom) MacLeod, 40 cm (16"), camel hair, vintage linen shepherds smock and handmade accessories. A limited edition of 10.

45

KARLA MAHANNA

Karla Mahanna Artist Bears

KARLA HAS LONG had a love affair with bears and was inspired to create her own from the old bears in her collection. Her love of the old-fashioned and love-worn bears is still very evident in her work today. She began bear-making in 1985, and first sold her bears while living in Saudi Arabia and then in Japan, mostly to friends and ex-pats. Originally from the United States, Karla now lives in Australia where she makes her bears full-time.

One of Australia's first professional bear artists, Karla still works alone. Nevertheless, she manages to make about 140 bears a year, with most of them being created as one-offs. Her favourite size to work on is from 40 cm (16") to 46 cm (18"). Her bears are distinguished by a rough-and-tumble worn-out antique look. They are often female and clothed in faded and stained dresses, lace and flowers. A degree in Fine Arts has trained her eye for meticulous detail. Karla sells both wholesale and retail, and attends about four or five shows a year. Karla Mahanna Artist Bears are hand-signed

and dated on the left paw.

Karla believes that the best bears cause you to fall in love with them at first sight, and hers certainly do that. She finds that her work is slowly evolving in one direction or another, and she hopes that her bears are becoming even more interesting as she grows with them.

Karla has won many top Australian awards, and has appeared in national magazines and Linda Mullins's recent book *Tribute to Teddy Bear Artists*. She feels lucky to be doing something she loves that is also financially rewarding, and she has certainly deserved her success.

For Karla, the least enjoyable part of bear-making is machining the pieces together, but this is far outweighed by the friends she has made through her bears and the satisfaction she feels in the creative act of making something that will hopefully touch someone's heart and life and bring them joy. Her advice to the struggling beginner is not to give up; success takes time and hard work. Her own problems have included moving around the world three times while she was trying to establish herself as a bear artist.

Karla says that 'making bears has brought me great peace and tranquillity and I hope that some of that passes on to the people who own my bears'.

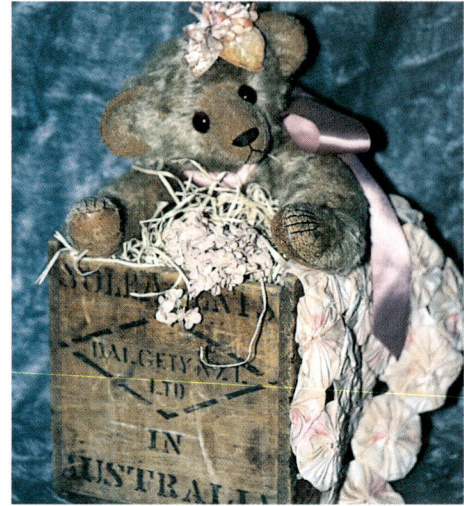

An 'Old Girl' in aged and distressed mohair. A clown bear, in hand-dyed and sparse mohair.

Karla and friends.

A group of Karla's bears in Alfonzo red and distressed mohair, with poly/pellet filling.

DENISE MATTHEWS

Denise & Friends Original Bears

*D*ENISE'S BEAR-MAKING career started in 1992 when some friends encouraged her to make a crazy patchwork bear. She made it in brown velvet from a *Family Circle* magazine pattern, and says, 'I still have and love that bear, even though it reminds me of how not to make one, with its joints in back-to-front, and its nose, eyes and ears all crooked and floppy'.

Through Karla Mahanna, Denise was introduced to the world of professional bear-making. Six months later she entered her first competition, won the section and has never looked back. She teaches patchwork, heirloom sewing and several other crafts at the Living and Learning Centre in her town of Diamond Creek. Her work has been published in the local newspaper, as well as in the Dutch bear magazine *Beer Bericht*.

Although she has always been a sewer, Denise decided to return to school to learn new skills that would

Denise with Lester, 36 cm (14"), in sparse mohair with sanded leather pawpads.

Rufus, 28 cm (11"), in red mohair clipped to look sparse.

assist her in her creativity. In 1994 she began an Associate Diploma of Visual Arts Design at her local college. In 1995 Denise is finding that she is spending more and more of her time designing and creating bears. She enjoys making one-of-a-kinds and her favourite size range to work within is from 30 cm (12") to 36 cm (14"). Her bears have a distinct look of yesteryear and often look a little worn. Denise's bears have a swing card giving their details, as well as a little patch sewn on their backsides with a signature and date.

The many shows in which Denise participates bring her great pleasure because of the friendships she makes with other bear-makers and the encouragement she receives from collectors. She says:

'One of the nicest compliments I have received was from a lady who had just recently been widowed. She fell in love with my bear called Bruno, but felt he was too expensive. Her daughters, observing the love affair, secretly bought the bear and some time later the lady returned to thank me. I know that Bruno helped the lady through her bad times and gave her much joy. It gives me great pleasure knowing that my bears go to wonderful homes and I hope to continue supplying quality bears.'

Belle, 43 cm (17"), in aged silk/alpaca fur with sanded leather pawpads and odd stitchs showing. A prize-winning antique reproduction bear.

Phoebe, 36 cm (14"), in aged mohair with aged leather pawpads, and Eden, 23 cm (9"), in sparse mohair.

MARGARET MICHEL

Original Bears By Margaret Michel

ARGARET MADE bears years ago for her children to grow up with, and in 1990 the urge to make another bear hit her again. After attending a doll and bear convention in 1991, she was determined to become not just a bear-maker but a bear artist. Margaret now sells her original designs through shows and shops as well as by special order, and, although she also has a full-time job, she makes up to 60 bears a year.

Mostly one-offs, Margaret's bears each have a fine gold thread daisy embroidered on their right pawpad as well as a small swing tag. They are all unclothed and many are made of hand-dyed mohair from natural dyes.

Margaret is working on her ideal bear, which is an old grizzly with a look of the wild about him, but until she is happy with her creation he won't be seen by the public. She enjoys taking her time with each bear and does not want to increase productivity at the expense of quality.

Clockwise from rear left: Ragtime, 35 cm (14"), in sparse gold mohair; Mintie, 30 cm (12"); Lavender, 15 cm (6"), in lavender-tipped mohair; Sunset, 23 cm (9"), in rose mohair; and Coaster, 25 cm (10"), in royal-blue mohair and named after the Gold Coast Eagles.

Margaret with Bruin, a one-off, and Minty, in hand-dyed mohair and only available when the dye plant is in season.

Tiffany, available in two sizes, 30 cm (12") and 35 cm (14"), in swirly mohair with pigskin pawpads and bootbutton eyes.

PATRICIA MULLINS

PATRICIA WAS ALREADY a well-known children's book illustrator and an authority in other craft areas before coming to the world of teddy bears. Having earned a Diploma in Graphic Design and a Fellowship in Illustration, Patricia also received a grant to study puppetry and animation overseas. She has won numerous awards, both in Australia and the United States, for children's book illustration, and has made a group of Fabulous Beast soft sculptures that have been exhibited all over Victoria, including in the National Gallery. Patricia is also known for her 'obsessive interest' in rocking horses and has written a major reference work on the topic, *The Rocking Horse; A History of Moving Toy Horses*, published in London in 1992.

She made her first toy at six, first sold her animal toys when she was 15, and made her first bear, a little Winnie the Pooh, 25 years ago. Patricia says that the first issue of the American magazine *Teddy Bear and Friends* inspired her even more, but until now she has not had the time to pursue bear-making.

The making of a koala for the competitions at the Sydney International Bear Fair in 1994 (where she won not only her Novice section, but also Best Overall) was Patricia's first public venture into toy-making, and also signalled a rediscovered direction.

Patricia's koalas have incredible life and personality, and are unlike any that have been made to date. Her work captures the imagination of all who see it, and it is hard to believe that she is just starting out in the world of bears. She feels her best achievements to date include her Fabulous Beasts, a large Blinky Bill koala and Muddleheaded Wombat made for Angus & Robertson's window displays, designing and making complete puppet shows and now developing and creating her koalas.

She feels she would like to be known for 'bears and animals that have a life of their own, are high quality, fully hand-crafted, Australian and limited editions or one-offs'. Patricia sees that all her work, whether writing about rocking horses, collecting toys, illustrating children's books or making bears and animals, is interlinked, involving childhood and toys, imagination and fantasy.

Patricia with some of her rocking horses.

Curly Gum the Koala, 40 cm (16"), in curly synthetic fur with felt pawpads and glass eyes. An open-mouth design based on real koalas rather than teddy bears. A prize-winner and Best Overall at the Sydney International Bear Fair 1994.

MARIA RIEDL

The Riedl Bear Collection

MARIA RECEIVED HER first real teddy, a Bully Bear designed by Peter Bull and made by the English toy company Nesbit, as late as 1982. She also received a storybook written and autographed by Peter Bull about his bears, and this began her love affair with teddies. In 1984 she first noticed the handmade bears of June Kittlety, and bought several for herself and her family in the United States. It wasn't until 1993, however, that Maria tried making bears, her first being an embroidered blanket-wool bear. She then made a patchwork bear and quickly started creating her own designs.

A painter in many mediums, Maria particularly enjoyed painting bears, but in 1994 she found that her artist bears started to outsell her bear paintings. A number of shops in Victoria and the United States now stock Maria's bears, and she also sells retail.

Born in Australia, Maria grew up in Canada and the United States, where she completed a teaching degree. On her return to Australia she worked as a specialist art teacher at primary school. She no longer teaches but has continued her own education, studying watercolour painting at Melbourne's RMIT and life drawing and oil painting at Mildura TAFE.

Maria now makes 75-100 bears a year and they range from one-offs to open editions. She used to dress her bears but now feels that minimal attire shows the bears as they are. Maria says her bears are also becoming less tubby, longer and more traditional. They are identified by a green ribbon backed onto a plaid ribbon with 'The Riedl Bear, Australia' and the year of manufacture embroidered in yellow. This is sewn onto the foot before the bear is made.

Like many artists, Maria sees her best achievement so far in her latest bear. Although she has only entered one competition, Maria took home two best teddy awards, and her bears have appeared in several publications and local newspapers.

While attending an Ashes test cricket match recently in Adelaide, Maria worked on a new bear, watched curiously by a tall Englishman next to her. When she finished her first Granville bear in front of his eyes, he exclaimed that he was a bear collector and had to have it. He couldn't leave behind a bear born during an Ashes test match! With some regret Maria watched him walk away clutching Granville, head and shoulders above the crowd, at the end of the day's play.

Maria loves her work, especially creating the bears' characters as she works their faces. She advises beginners to make sure their joints are tight and the stuffing is firm. Maria attended four shows in 1994 and plans to attend 10 in 1995.

A group of Maria's mohair bears, from 36 cm (14") to 61 cm (24"), with a painting of hers in the background.

Maria with a range of her Granville bears.

ADELE ROWE

The Serendipity Collection

*I*N 1984 ADELE was inspired to create a small teddy by a close friend and porcelain doll-maker, Carolyn Dixon:

'She felt her dolls needed a companion and asked me if I would make a small bear as an accessory. I have always had an interest in miniatures and took on the challenge. My first bear was awful ... so awful in fact that I gave it to a Cabbage Patch Doll! But soon I was happy with my creations, and thus began my enchantment with miniature bear-making.'

Adele enjoys making bears of 7.5 cm (3") and under, and her work tends to be feminine without being too fussy. Until recently her bears had a label attached to them reading 'Handmade by Adele ... born in Australia'. Over the last year they have had a suede heart, initialed 'A', on their bottoms. Adele and her bears were recently showcased in the *Australian Country Craft 1994 Annual,* and have also appeared in other Australian bear and craft magazines.

In June 1994, Adele and her husband opened The Serendipity Collection, Australia's first full-time teaching studio for bear-making with a full range of bear-making supplies. They also have a bear artist gallery, sell collectables and crafts, as well as an 'Orphan Bear Adoption Centre', which is a mini museum of old bears rescued from a variety of unpleasant situations. Adele finds little time to make bears now, and often gets her 'fix' from her students and their delight at their new creations. Even so, she still manages to make up to 40 bears a year, and they are much prized by collectors.

McDuff, 40 cm (16"), in swirly mohair with a yes/no mechanism and a music box; and Strawbeary, 28 cm (11"), in hand-dyed mohair with a cream base. Both one-offs.

Nutmeg, 7 cm (2¾"), a limited edition in short-pile mohair, with his little friend.

Adele with a hug of her bears.

DEBBIE SARGENTSON

Nostalgia Bears

ITTLE DID I KNOW when I was seven years old and making cloth rabbits and unjointed teddy bears with my nanna on her treadle Singer sewing machine that I would be creating teddy bears again 23 years on.' Debbie's reunion with the teddy bear began in May 1993 when she left full-time employment as a human resources manager to take a short career break. Her background in sewing, pattern-drafting and craftwork gave her the basic know-how, so Debbie decided to try making a bear. It wasn't long before the Nostalgia Bear started to take shape.

After taking first place in her first show competition and being approached by a number of bear shops who wanted to stock her bears, Debbie was sold on bear-making. Nostalgia Bears grew into a full-time business, with her bears winning numerous awards and appearing in Australian, American and English bear magazines.

Nostalgia Bears is a solo operation, with Debbie doing everything from concept design to finished bear. She finds, however, her mother's support, opinion and assistance, particularly before a big show, to be invaluable. Attention to detail means that Nostalgia Bears are few in quantity, with no more than 120 being made each year, yet high in quality. The bears are one-of-a-kinds or small limited editions, with sizes from 30 cm (12'') upwards. Debbie also accepts a small number of specially dressed privately commissioned bears, each of which can take up to 100 hours to complete.

Debbie's bears are known for their old-world appearance, particularly their large ears and long limbs, as well as their antique accessories and clothing. Her signature on their right foot and tag on their back provide formal identification of an original Nostalgia Bear.

Nostalgia Bears now appear on Bear Hugs greeting cards and a limited edition range of hand-painted teddy-bear shirts. Debbie stocks a handful of bear specialist shops around Australia and attends four or five shows in New South Wales and Victoria each year.

'The shows I attend give collectors an opportunity to acquire a bear direct from the artist and give me a chance to meet them, gain valuable feedback and perhaps inspiration. Working on my own when I'm creating my bears can be isolating, a feeling I'm sure most bear artists and makers can relate to.'

Nostalgia Bears have been sold in many countries, and in 1994 Debbie went to several shows in the United States and England with her bears, where they were well received. She believes the exposure to the overseas markets was a tremendous experience and a great inspiration to continue to try different designs that depart from the traditional teddy bear. Shortly afterwards, Debbie launched her new range of Grizzly bears, which have already won both prizes and recognition.

Grizzlies Marmaduke and Junior, 61 cm (24'') and 25 cm (10''), in sparse mohair with glass eyes, a limited edition of 75

Debbie with some of her creations.

Joshua and Teddy, 48 cm (19'') and 20 cm (8''), a one-of-a-kind in sparse mohair and handmade outfit.

ATHANS STEFFEN

Steffen Bears

*I*N JULY 1993 ATHANS saw a television programme featuring Jennifer Laing and her bears, and decided to give bear-making a try. Within three months Athans had created her own designs, and was selling to several bear shops as well as to overseas customers in Japan. (One Japanese collector now has eight of Athans' bears in her collection.)

Athans now makes around 200 bears a year in what has fast become a full-time job for her. She does all the work herself, although her husband helps with the stuffing when there are deadlines to meet. Her executive background has helped Athans in the business and marketing side of her venture, as she is experienced in budgeting and liaising wth people.

She enjoys making 30 cm (12") to 50 cm (20'') bears most, but her style changes over time as she experiments. (Athans thinks her motto should be 'Keep everyone guessing'.) Steffen Bears have a tag with their logo and Athans' name sewn into their back seam.

Athans attends only two shows a year and is in the process of changing many aspects of her bear business, including scaling down her wholesale orders and concentrating on her own retailing. She believes in tenacity and a fear of the unknown, which she says keeps her going in her chosen profession.

Bluey, 36 cm (14"), in blue sparse English mohair, a limited edition of 10.

Borjolais, 36 cm (14"), in wine-coloured sparse English mohair, a limited edition of 10.

(Left) Athans holding Fitzwilliam, 43 cm (17"), in feathered German mohair wearing a hand-knitted sweater, a limited edition of five.

Mr Honey, 20 cm (8"), in beige and gold mohair with leather pawpads and a bee motif waistcoat.

Mr H. Chestnut, 20 cm (8"), in wool with felt inner ears and pawpads, and a black waistcoat.

INES COOK

What Ho Bears

INES FIRST TRIED bear-making about five years ago, having always enjoyed hand-sewing and embroidery. Her first customers were her family and friends, but Ines now makes 40 bears a year at what is a part-time job for her. She likes the look of a well-used traditional bear, but tries to add a little something different to her own bears. Ines enjoys making bears in many different sizes, and loves matching colours and shades of materials and furs. She puts handmade labels into her bears and sells them herself at the couple of shows she attends each year.

Ines has a number of tips for producing a good bear:
1. Choose materials carefully and always match the fabric nap.
2. Be precise when drawing and cutting patterns.
3. Be precise and neat when sewing.
4. Be slow and meticulous when stuffing.
5. Pay particular attention to the things you like doing least.

Recently, Ines has been using many talents to write and illustrate a collection of children's stories, based on a set of six characters that she created. The stories revolve around Mr H. Chestnut (see picture). Ines has used poetry and humour to stimulate a sense of magic and love in children for all things in nature.

Ines with one of her bears.

HELEN ACKROYD

My Bear

HELEN MADE HER first bear in 1994, after being inspired by a pamphlet advertising bear-making classes. She quickly began to sell to bear retailers in Perth, and found that the stores were very helpful with suggestions on marketing and presenting her bears. Helen says she has acquired her bear-making skills by trial and error, as well as by buying all the bear-making books on the market!

Working alone from home, Helen makes between 50 and 100 bears a year. She finds that handling fur between December and March, when the temperatures in Perth can reach 40° to 45°C, is out of the question, but works hard at bear-making for the rest of the year. Helen is fortunate in that her husband, who is a professional sales agent, does most of her wholesale selling for her. Her favourite size to work on is around 40 cm (16″), and My Bears have a blue on white tag sewn in the seam under the arm.

'I would like people to think that my bears will not fall apart in the first wash and that they are safe for a child to cuddle while alone in bed or anywhere else for that matter. I think most of all that I would like my bears to fill that space in the human heart.'

Morris, 42 cm (16¼″), in natural English mohair, a limited edition of 10.

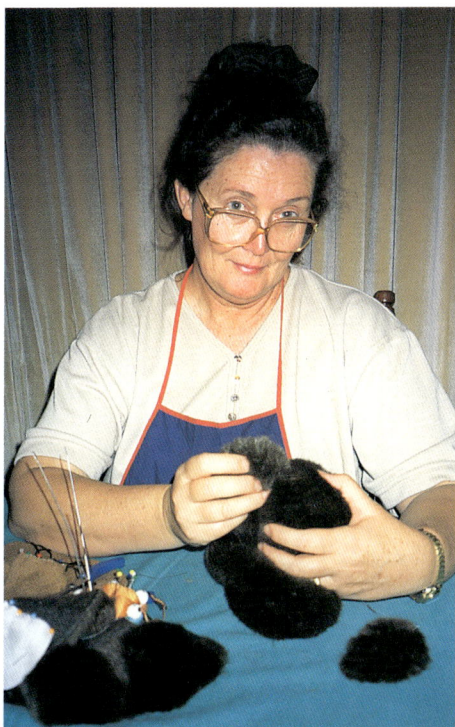

Helen at work.

Raffles, 32 cm (12¼″), in gold German mohair, a limited edition of 10.

LINDA DAVIDSON
Bramble Bears

IN 1991 LINDA read a magazine article about a woman making jointed traditional bears out of old wool coats and mohair. After tracking down her mohair supplies, Linda made her first bear. The next day she found herself making her second bear, and was surprised when orders for her bears started to flow in. Linda has all the necessary skills for successful bear-making, for as well as having formal training in textiles, she has been involved in other fabric crafts since childhood.

Apart from her husband's occasional help with cutting out and stuffing, Linda works alone and spends about three-quarters of her time making bears. She makes roughly 100 a year, half of which are one-offs and half open editions, and sells both retail and wholesale. Bramble Bears have an embroidered name tag in their back seams, as well as a detailed swing tag.

Linda also teaches bear-making locally, and her work has appeared in national bear magazines.

Although Linda says she does not look too far ahead, she has made a bear for the future:

'I had a woman who gave me a time capsule (a small metal cylinder containing personal information and mementos) to insert into a bear I was making for her so that it would be discovered by future generations.

Siblings Alexander and Alexandra (wearing a hand-smocked linen dress), 43 cm (17"), in curly German mohair with glass eyes and suede pawpads.

Linda with Bruno, 54 cm (21½"), in German feather-tip mohair with suede pawpads.

Good friends Edward and Edwina, 53 cm (21"), in distressed German mohair with glass eyes and suede pawpads, wearing handmade outfits.

DAWN GIBBON

Busselton Bears

TED MENTON'S BOOK *The Teddy Bear Lover's Companion* provided the inspiration for Dawn to begin making bears, which she first did in 1992 for her grandson. In August 1994 she started selling through a local gallery, and her bear-making has now become a full-time occupation, with all her bears selling through two local stores.

Working entirely by hand, Dawn finds that each of her bears takes about 20 hours to make. She feels she is fortunate in having a very supportive husband, as she spends up to 50 hours a week working on her bears, all of which are one-offs. Her aim is to make about 100 a year. The bear she loved as a child had a growl, and so Dawn tends to give most of her bears a voice. Each Busselton Bear has a label, green on white, on his right foot as well as a handwritten swing tag and birth certificate.

'As there is a sad lack of bear fairs and events in Western Australia, I have not entered my bears in competitions, but recently a club has been formed in Perth called Arctophiles of WA, so I hope that things will change in the near future.'

Bruno, in brown synthetic, with Theodore, in gold mohair, and Hugo, in beige synthetic. All 50 cm (20").

Dawn with James and Belinda

James and Belinda, 46 cm (18"), in beige mohair.

MICHELLE AND JULIE HYLAND

Hyland Bears – Australia

THE ONLY SISTER duo on the bear scene in Australia, Michelle and Julie come from a creative family and have always made things together. Michelle has a Bachelor of Arts, majoring in Fine Arts, and Julie was well on her way to a similar degree when an addictive interest in bears cut short her studies. The sisters made their first bear (which their mum still has) from a Gooseberry Hill pattern in November 1991, and they quickly understood how a bear pattern worked and what could be changed. Sheer enjoyment drove them on and within a few months they had bears for sale in a local clothing shop.

Their interest has turned into a full-time career for both of them. In fact, Hyland Bears have become so popular that Michelle and Julie rely on their mum to help with the sewing (because they know how beautifully she sews) and also employ a few experienced stuffers. Their dedication and teamwork show in the fact that in 1994 alone Hyland Bears – Australia produced around 640 bears. Mainly sold wholesale, their bears are found all over Australia, Singapore and Germany.

Blackbeard the Pirate, 50 cm (20"), a prize-winning bear in mohair with mohair rovings, velvet, linen and suede with a broom-handle peg-leg.

Reuben, 61 cm (24"), with Jingle, Sore Bear, Baby Bear, 18 cm (7"), and Harvey. All limited editions in mohair. Jingles has bells in his tummy.

Initially Hyland Bears were mostly open editions because too many people wanted the same bear. Now the sisters prefer to do one-offs and small editions, which allow them more scope in their designing and creating. They find that each sister has a certain designing and sewing style, and that the individual looks are becoming more marked, but they enjoy the differences and help each other out. Both are influenced by the early long-limbed and lifelike German bears, and they hold a vision of the ideal bear as 'a bear so special that its appeal outlasts its generation and continues to enchant and mystify the next, like Teddy Girl'.

When Hyland Bears began in 1991 Michelle and Julie were lino-printing their own fabric name tags on the right foot (or under the left arm on a small bear), and using recycled cardboard swing tags. They followed these with professionally printed cream fabric tags and parchment paper swing tags. Now

Michelle and Julie Hyland with their favourites: Happy Birthday (limited edition) and Samuel (open edition), 46 cm (18") and 43 cm (17"), in mohair with safety glass eyes.

they use cream cloth woven tags (maroon for their limited editions) and cream card swing tags. They keep records of all their bears in a series of record books.

The sisters have won many prizes for their bears and their work has been seen in publications and on television, but they believe their best achievement is the fact that they still love working on bears every day. In 1994 they attended three shows, and hope to do only two in 1995. They have taught many bear-making classes in and around their home state, as well as in Sydney, and have even taught an 'interesting' class of non-English-speaking Germans in Dortmund, Germany.

For Michelle and Julie, there are few aspects of bear-making that they don't enjoy. The pleasure they get out of their creativity and the people they meet in the business makes it all worth their while. They would like to be known to have created things that their kids can keep for their kids.

Bear-making has already taken them around the world, and Julie and Michelle plan to continue travelling as far as their bears will take them.

FAY MALONEY

Fay M Bears

A DRESSMAKING TEACHER for many years, Fay subsequently taught textile and embroidery crafts and finally was the owner of a specialist needlecraft shop in Melbourne, before retiring in 1990 to enjoy what she thought would be an easier life. Fay made her first bears in January 1991 to replace a lost childhood bear. She did not intend to sell her work, but after lending some of the bears for a charity exhibition she was surprised by requests from collectors. Her bear business just grew from there.

Far from retiring to a quieter life, Fay now often has to work seven days a week to keep up with the workload, and in 1994 made 180 bears. She works alone and feels that she has to make the entire bear herself to be happy with the result. Many of Fay's bears are one-offs and small limited editions, although she does also do a few open editions. Her designs range from 15 cm (6") to 90 cm (36"), but at the moment Fay enjoys making smaller bears from 15 cm (6") to 23 cm (9").

Feeling that she would rather make bears than market them, Fay sells mostly wholesale with some mail orders. She has found some marvellous shops that are very supportive of her work. She now has the time to attend only one show each year, and she has entered only one competition (where she won two awards), as she prefers judging to competing. She sees this as a hangover from her teaching background of encouraging others to try. Her work has been covered in both international bear magazines and books, but Fay thinks that the best aspect of bear-making for her has been the wonderful people she has met and the friends she has made.

Fay found that initially her love of antique bears influenced her work, but now believes her later designs are more innovative while still retaining the appealing traditional qualities. Fay M

Bears are identified by a hand-worked cross-stitch label attached to the right foot pad as well as a swing tag. As her swing tag says, her bears are 'created with loving care'.

Outback Santa, 25 cm (10"), a one-off in multicoloured mohair, on a wooden bike.

Fay Maloney holding Leschenaultia, 46 cm (18"), in mohair with sailor-girl outfit.

Treacle, 38 cm (15"), an open-edition bear in country-style mohair; and Willie, 50 cm (20"), a limited edition of eight in feathered mohair with a waistcoat.

JAN HANLON

IN MAY 1993 Jan was idly browsing in a bookshop when she saw a book on bear-making and decided to try it for herself. She has never looked back. She believes that growing up with strong parental encouragement in all things arty and crafty helped her along in her chosen path. Within a few months Jan was selling at her first show where she was a successful 'table filler' for her doll-making sister, Susie McMahon.

Apart from working a few hours a week in a local craft shop, Jan devotes all her time to making her bears, producing around 400 a year. Most of her bears are open editions, with about 15 per cent being one-offs. Her favourite size range is from 20 cm (8") to 40 cm (16"), and her bears sell both wholesale and retail. They each have an oval leather or ultrasuede foot label bearing Jan's monogram and year they were made.

Jan attends up to 10 doll, bear and craft shows a year and also teaches her craft. She is pleased that bear-making has enabled her to quit the nine-to-five office grind and work at something that she loves.

Natasha, 40 cm (16"), in distressed German mohair with leather pawpads, metal eyes and floppy poly/pellet filling. From Jan's range of 'old bears'.

Little Ben 33 cm (13"), in German mohair, leather pads and glass eyes. Little Will 33 cm (13") also in German mohair but with metal eyes. Both are fully jointed.

Mama Bear, 33 cm (13"), in brown German mohair with bootbutton eyes and a hand-crocheted collar. Tibbs, 25 cm (10"), in sparse German mohair with bootbutton eyes.

(Left) Jan with Tibbs, 25 cm (10"), in sparse German mohair with bootbutton eyes.

MARIANNE HOWE

Omi's Bears

*W*ANTING TO MAKE a teddy bear for her first grandson prompted Marianne to look for a pattern in bear magazines, where she was inspired by an article on Sylvana McAuliffe's miniature bears. She was determined to try miniatures and, after learning the bear basics in 1991, she scaled down her patterns till her bears ranged from 4 cm (1½") to 18 cm (7"). Marianne started selling her bears in 1992 at a local bear shop, but it was not until she moved to Tasmania in the same year that bear-making became her career.

Marianne hand-stitches all her bears and makes about 250 a year. Her husband helps with the jointing, using a system that Marianne devised with small nylon buttons and cotter pins, or split pins. Omi's Bears are all open editions with about 20 in Marianne's catalogue. They all have a swing tag and, since the beginning of 1995, also a leather tag in their back seams giving Marianne's initials, the date and their name, 'Omi's Bears'.

Marianne's bears find homes all over the world, and have appeared in Australian and English bear magazines, as well as winning many prizes. Marianne is now so busy with fulfilling her orders, along with attending several shows each year and teaching workshops, that she seldom has time to make bears to sell through shops.

'Recently I gave a one-on-one work-shop with a lady who combined a holiday in Tasmania with spending a full day with me to make one of my bears. I enjoyed myself as much as she did, as I had plenty of time to pass on lots of little tips. I really enjoy giving workshops as I remember only too well the frustrating times when I started to make small bears and I had no-one to ask.'

Clockwise from left rear: Wellington, in pink and in gold mohair, and Gordon, in curly cotton, both 17 cm (6½"); Franklin in spiky mohair, Jean in extra sparse mohair and Little Brompton in mohair, all 13 cm (5").

Marianne and her little Omi's Bears.

Forget Me Not, 5.5 cm (2¼"), in upholstery plush. First prize-winner at the Sydney International Bear Fair 1994.

The Gang (left to right): Small Heritage Bear, Benson (back), Terry, Original, Worn Bear, Woppy, Large Heritage Bear and Cubby. All in different mohair, from 23 cm (9") to 50 cm (20").

SHARYN AND DAVID HUTCHINS

Brookside Bears

As BEAR COLLECTORS living in a small state, Sharyn and David found it difficult to find quality artist bears. They saw a gap in the market in Tasmania and thought they would try to fill it. Sharyn first started making bears at a class in 1992 and when David saw that she was having so much fun he decided to give it a try too. They first started selling their bears to friends and colleagues and then at the Salamanca Market in Hobart and a couple of small shops.

At the moment Sharyn and David make about 50 bears a year, and do it as a team effort:

'David is usually the one who comes up with the great ideas. I can also tell him that I want a pattern for a certain type of bear and he can usually come up with something for me. We then work on the fine tuning and finishing off together, and we both have equal input. I think this is great for the quality of the workmanship too, as we are each other's number one critic. David is really good with the tough nuts and bolts stuff too.'

Sharyn and David hope eventually to make this a full-time career. They produce a mixture of one-offs, limited editions and open editions, but even the open editions are very small. They find that they have so many design ideas that David is drawing up the new patterns before Sharyn can finish the last one. They prefer to work between 23 cm (9") and 40 cm (16"), and sell both retail and wholesale. Brookside Bears have brown leather sewn-in labels with gold foil printing, and swing tags giving the individual details for each bear.

Their vision of the ideal bear is one who stands out from the crowd, and they see their work as blending the old with the new. They aim for their bears to be a little different while retaining the timeless appeal of a classic bear.

Their advice is just to 'put your heart into your designs and the rest will follow', and their main frustration is finding that there are not enough hours in the day. 'We are not seeking fame and fortune, we enjoy doing this together as a team, and would just like to spread a little happiness to those who love bears.'

Sharyn with one of their latest designs, Worn Bear.

BOB WHITE

Bob's Bears

MAKING BEARS IS a bit like having an incurable addiction. You make one to see if you can do it, than you make another because the next one will be better than the first. My addiction is now over 10 years old, and I made my 1000th bear just before last Christmas.'

From a childhood filled with toys, many of which his parents had made for him, Bob now in turn makes toys for his children. Originally trained as an art teacher and with a background in woodworking, welding and sculpture, he found that visualising things came easily to him. Bob made his first bear from a piece of leftover saddlecloth fur fabric. The bears quickly took over his life. Even so, Bob does not consider himself a collector. Nor does he have a stock of bears around, as he usually works to order, unless he is working on some new ideas or new materials. He sees his work as constantly evolving and is not sure if he would recognise one of his own bears from five years ago.

Bob's Bears are mostly small limited editions, with the exception of his very popular Clancy; a mountain stockman complete with 'oilskin' coat, leather hat and plaited whip, whose edition is now over 120. Bob's bears are essentially masculine (he says he is incapable of making a female bear), usually between 43 cm (17") and 58 cm (23") and often dressed simply to emphasise their characters. Each bear has the Bob's Bears logo printed on one foot and is often also numbered and signed.

Bob loves attending shows and seeing the faces of people who come across a bear for the first time. 'This is something every bear-maker should do. All creative people see their creation happening but never see the end result for the first time such as people do at a show.'

The Honorable Angus, 46 cm (18"), in swirly German mohair with glass eyes, a woven safety nose and the ancient hunting Ogilvie tartan.

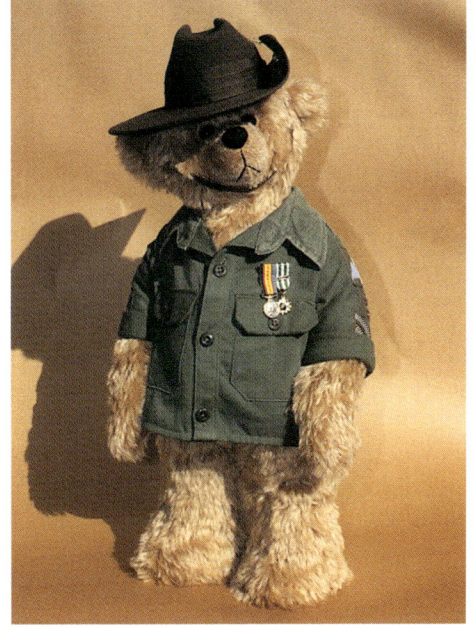

Staff Sargeant Albert McBear, 58 cm (23"), in buff mohair with glass eyes and a woven safety nose, a genuine Akubra slouch hat, army shirt, medals and badges.

Bob with The Aviator, 47 cm (18.5"), and his aircraft.

The Reader, 58 cm (23"), in French acrylic fur with glass eyes and a woven safety nose.

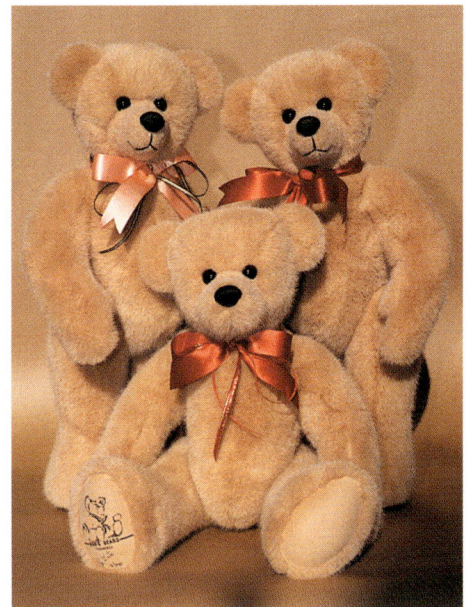

ANNE BOOTH

Chadwick Bears

ANNE'S INTRODUCTION to the world of bears occurred when she first bought a bear for herself, 'not because I wanted to buy a bear, it just said, "Take me home"'. From then on she became interested in the power of teddy bears, and as she had always sewn (and had spent many years making patchwork quilts) it seemed natural for her to make some bears of her own. Anne first started making them in October 1992, and she was selling them and winning prizes for them shortly afterwards.

In spite of having a part-time job Anne spends a lot of time making bears, which she does alone, and produces around 75 a year. Most of them are open editions, with some limited editions and one-offs. Her favourite sizes are in the 7.5 cm (3") to 18 cm (7") range, but she does make bears up

Fisher Bear, 12 cm (4¾"), in German synthetic with fishing accessories. The same bear also comes as a skier, golfer, tennis player and other sporting characters.

Ben, 7.5 cm (3"), in longer pile upholstery velvet with hat and scarf, a limited edition of four.

Anne with Eloise and Christopher, both 40 cm (16"), open editions in antiqued wool.

to 40 cm (16"). Anne sells her bears both wholesale and retail and attends several shows each year. She has won many prizes at shows around New Zealand, and one of her bears fetched over $1000 at a charity auction.

Anne's bears are traditional in style, but many wear hats, vests or accessories and some of her bears have poseable armature. One of her latest miniature bears has internal wiring to make him more poseable. All Chadwick Bears have a sewn-in label and a logo swing tag.

Anne sees her work as constantly improving and is always interested in trying new materials. She finds great satisfaction in seeing that a new design is successful. Although she enjoys all aspects of bear-making, she often wants to finish the basic sewing quickly so that she can concentrate on the face and personality. She is pleased that as her bears are becoming better known more and more work is coming in, giving her the opportunity to develop both her business and her ideas.

Left to right: Hearthrob, Clown with balloon, Dinks, Brian and Clown. All 7 cm (2¾"), except Brian, who is 10 cm (4"), in upholstery fabric and open editions.

SANDY COOMBS

Sandy's Bears

SANDY BECAME AN arctophile from the moment she first walked into a bear shop in 1985, and took the step from collector to maker in 1991 when she attended a bear class by Jennifer Laing in Sydney. In 1994, when she had confidence in her creations, she began full-time bear-making. At the same time she returned to New Zealand. Sandy began to sell her little bears to friends and approached retail outlets. She now sells some of her output of 150 bears a year to specialist bear shops in both Australia and New Zealand.

Sandy's bears are around 13 cm (5"), which is the size that 'fits perfectly in a hand'. She collects miniatures and thinks that the smaller bears are cute and easy to transport and display.

Completely hand-stitched, her bears are always smiling and come with a small black and gold on white swing tag giving their details. Sandy takes both wholesale and retail orders, and is becoming well known for the care and time she puts into each and every bear.

Sandy is happy doing what she loves and is constantly experimenting with her work. 'Living on a farm, away from the distractions of city life, I now have the perfect environment for making my bears.'

Sandy with two tiny friends.

Ruffles and Twinkle, both 13 cm (5"), in German mohair, with little Truffle, 10 cm (4"), in upholstery fabric. All open editions and prize-winners.

65

JUDITH HARDY

Lancewood Bears

JUDITH WAS A KEEN doll-maker until an artist bear in a magazine turned her head in 1990. Bear-making is not a full-time occupation for her at present, but she hopes eventually to let it take over her life. Even part-time, Judith still manages to make over 200 bears a year, working by herself.

All Lancewood Bears are limited editions and range from 9 cm (3½") to 66 cm (26") in size. Available both wholesale and retail, the bears each have identifying tie-on labels. Judith's prize-winning creations have appeared in local papers as well as at the annual show she attends.

One of Judith Hardy's bears, 25 cm (10"), a limited edition in German mohair.

JANIS HARRIS

Almost South Pole

WITH A BACKGROUND as a professional dress designer and tailor, Janis had many skills to draw on when she first saw an artist bear in a shop in 1993 and wanted to make her own. In 1994 she exhibited at a doll show and since then has been working full-time at her bear-making.

Creating mostly one-offs and small limited editions, and working alone, Janis has lost count of the number of bears she has made. She works in sizes up to 1.5 m (5 ft), but prefers the 25 cm (10") to 46 cm (18") range. Almost South Pole bears can be identified by their woven label machine-stitched on their back, below the head. Most of them are sold retail.

Also a doll-maker, Janis has received several notable New Zealand awards for her work including an Idex Award and a Silver Rose Award. Her bears have also appeared in many international bear magazines.

Janis goes to as many shows as she can manage, both locally and internationally, and her bears can be found in just as many parts of the world. One of her bears was taken to the little village in Denmark that her great-grandfather had left to emigrate to New Zealand. Another, called Travelbear, has been all over the world with his owners, who won't leave home without him.

Willy, 50 cm (20"), in hand-dyed distressed mohair with glass eyes and leather pawpads. A one-of-a-kind.

Janis Harris with a very large friend.

Spotty Dick, 36 cm (14"), made from an old plush coat, with bootbutton eyes. A limited edition of two.

Sugar Sack Sid, 38 cm (15"), made from a hand-dyed old sugar sack, with a hand-dyed jerkin. Open edition, depending on fabric availability.

ROSE HILL

Rose Hill Bears

AFTER FORMAL training in the arts, Rose says she 'graduated to bear-making' after a five-year apprenticeship in porcelain dolls. Her first bear design was for a doll convention in 1987, when a hundred chubby little unjointed bears with tails were made by Harrisons (then a New Zealand company). Her first 'real' bear came afterwards when, with Dawn Nicholl's (Greawaki Bears) encouragement, Rose attempted her first jointed bear:

'He went through untold metamorphoses over several months, until finally I got one I was happy with. "Eureka", I thought and, somewhat confused, attributed the saying to Einstein, so Einstein Bears were born. I still use this name on the bears I make myself.'

Until 1992, Rose sold her Einstein Bears through her shop 'Victorian Rose'. Now she sells her bears through selected retail outlets in both New Zealand and Australia, and through the shows that she attends. The New Zealand fur fabric importers Furtex Ltd distribute patterns that she designs for them. Rose also designs for Bear with Us, a New Zealand soft toy manufacturer that sells worldwide. As well as designing and making bears, Rose teaches, writes and runs the Midwinter Doll & Teddy Bear Festival in Auckland each year.

Rose's work has been showcased in newspapers and magazines, and she has appeared with her bears on Australian television a couple of times.

Her personal bear output varies, but she makes between 100 and 150 bears a year. Most are one-offs and she says her low boredom threshold seldom allows a limited edition to get past 10, even if the original intention was 25. Her

Rose Hill with William, the 46 cm (18") mascot bear for the International Rugby Hall of Fame.

limited edition bears often have tails. Rose's favourite size is 30 cm (12"), although she will make a bear as small as 15 cm (6") and has been known to make them as large as 2 m (6½ ft). Until 1995 Rose put paper tags on her one-off bears and sewn-in burgundy labels on limited edition bears. Since 1994 most also have had a cream or a pink neck ribbon printed with 'Victorian Rose' and 'Einstein Bears'.

Rose sees her best achievement so far

('apart from surviving parenthood') as her Willie Bear, the mascot for the International Rugby Hall of Fame in Auckland. The 500 in the inaugural collectors' edition are in German distressed mohair, assembled by Bear with Us and hand-finished by Rose. They are authentically dressed, boxed, signed and numbered. A smaller, plush version of Willie Bear is also made for the tourist trade.

The biggest problem Rose has had with her bear-making occurred when she had a disagreement with her washing machine over dying mohair. She now hand-dyes in the bath. As for the least enjoyable part of bear-making, Rose says that 'vacuuming is the price you pay for the pleasure of making bears!'.

'Last year a dear arctophile friend of mine was very sick, so I took a small bear to keep her company after my visit to the hospital. Sadly, she passed away a few days later. Many of her bears came to the funeral, but I didn't see that little one among them. I thought that perhaps she had left it to the hospital toy libary, where she had worked. It wasn't until a month later I discovered that she had actually taken it with her!'

Barrie, 46 cm (18"), a one-off bear in hand-dyed mohair with velour pawpads.

Casper and Cranberry, both 30 cm (12") and one-of-a-kinds.

Heather with Myles, 48 cm (19"), in mohair with a leather collar and growler.

Gilbert, 53 cm (21"), a one-off in mohair with flock and pellet filling.

HEATHER LYELL

D'Lyell Bears

HEATHER IS A BEAR collector who has become so absorbed in the bear world that she and her husband now have their own retail bear business. It all began when Heather made her first bear while she was at home sick one day. She was so keen to finish him that when she realised she didn't have any stuffing she cut up her husband's old pants and used them.

Heather's bears are in various styles, which she labels as 'serious' or old-fashioned bears, 'fun' bears with quirky expressions often made out of unusual materials, and 'Bears of Yesteryear', a series of elderly travellers. Her identifying mark is a small ladybird button sewn onto the bear in various places.

After setting herself up selling her bears at local shows, she was surprised at the number of enquiries regarding materials and supplies. She knew from her own experience that there was no-one selling everything under one roof in her area, so took the plunge from being a bank manager to being a bear shop owner. Bear Essentials opened in Auckland in November 1992, and stocks everything from supplies to collectable artist bears and accessories.

The success of the store has meant that Heather's bear-making has slowed down, but she still manages to make around 80 bears a year. 'As Bear Essentials grows and takes on a staff member or two then hopefully I will have more time to do what I enjoy most, the designing and making of teddy bears.'

Aunt Mabel, from the Bears of Yesteryear series, 53 cm (21"), a one-off in mohair with clothes, undergarments, and accessories including a fully stocked handbag.

FRANCES MCLEARY

Braidwood Bears

FRANCES NEVER HAD a childhood bear, and the thought of making herself a fur bear to display with some old toys was enough to prompt her to begin. She had originally envisaged a girl bear with smocked dress and bonnet but her first bear was definitely male, so Frances altered her designs to achieve a look that has become her style.

In her five years of bear-making Frances has won many prizes and her bears have been well received. She makes anywhere between 300 and 400 bears a year, fitting the work in around teaching horticulture at a local polytechnic. She creates the bears and their clothing on her own, but her husband helps with the joints and in making any wooden accessories the bears might need.

All Braidwood Bears have a blue ribbon tag sewn into the lower back seam stating 'Braidwood Bears, original designs by Frances McLeary in New Zealand', as well as a swing tag giving their details. All are photographically recorded and numbered.

Frances attends three or four shows a year in New Zealand and in 1994 travelled to Sydney for the first International Bear Fair. She hopes to travel to the United States one day, but for now is happy to explore her bears' developing characters.

(Above) Storytime with Poppa, a three-bear one-of-a-kind set: Poppa, 61 cm (4"), and Pippa, 30 cm (12"), holding a 7.5 cm (3") toy bear. All in plush with safety eyes.

Frances with some of the Flowergirls.

(Right) Bledisloe, 61 cm (24"), a limited edition of five in two types of plush fur with suede pawpads and safety eyes, wearing the All Blacks team outfit.

SYNDI MUIR

Muir Bears

*T*HE BIRTH OF her daughter in 1991 inspired Syndi to make her first bear. She had fond memories of her own childhood Steiff bears, but she wanted to give her daughter something truly special. After quickly picking up the bear-making habit Syndi started selling her bears in a local store in Hawaii, which she still does even though she now lives in New Zealand.

Syndi makes less than 80 bears a year, in what is a full-time occupation. Most are limited editions, and she loves incorporating old lace, fabrics, ribbons and buttons into her work. Syndi finds she works best switching between miniatures and larger bears of 28 cm (11") to 33 cm (13"). She sells both wholesale and direct to collectors. All her bears have a 'Muir' tag giving their year of make.

'Over time I've been able to work smaller and also create a wider range of dressed miniatures. I have a small book filled with ideas for 'bears to be' and I don't think I'll ever run out of ideas.'

A 43 cm (17") feather-finish mohair bear with Spanish suede paws and glass eyes.

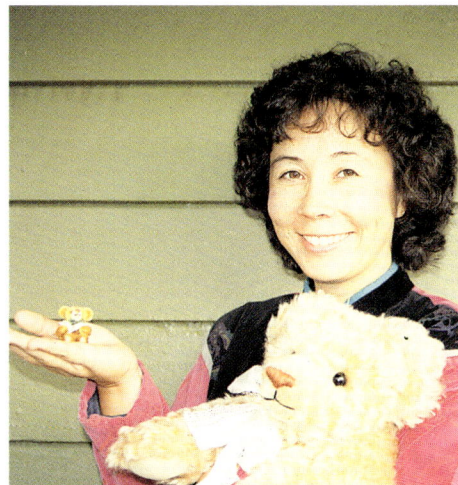

Syndi with a 43 cm (17") mohair bear and a miniature 5 cm (2") bear from her range of Muir Bears.

Victorian ladies, 6 cm (2½") tall in white velvet with ultrasuede pawpads, onyx bead eyes and antique lace and ribbon outfits.

SARA MURRAY

Bear Looms

SARA BOUGHT SOME teddy bear kits at a local craft show one wet weekend in early 1994, and made them both before the weekend was over. She started experimenting with her own designs ('I ended up with some bears that only a mother would love!'), and by August 1994 felt she was ready to try selling them. She now stocks a bear shop in Auckland as well as receiving orders from overseas. Bear Looms bears have a gold on black tag sewn into the back seam.

Sara's creative background has paid off well for her, and she plans on expanding her production when she gives up her full-time position in an advertising agency to have her first child in late 1995 Up until now Sara's bears have all been one-offs, but she intends to make some limited editions as she gets more involved in shows. Although she works alone, her husband, Andrew, insists he helps out by naming every bear when it's finished.

(Above) Charlotte, 40 cm (16"), a one-off in mohair with glass eyes and poly/pellet stuffing.
(Below) Podge, 40 cm (16"), a one-off in mohair with glass eyes and cotton stuffing.

Sara holding Hastings, 38 cm (15"), in distressed mohair with glass eyes and cotton/pellet stuffing. A limited edition of five.

72

Drizzel, 62 cm (24½"), and Pink Baby, both one-offs. Fully jointed, in handmade hand-moulded felt.

Mrs. Tattybutton, a Bidibid bear, 40 cm (16"), a one-off in mohair with antique lace and beads.

Trunk, 29 cm (11½"), fully jointed, in handmade hand-moulded felt. A determined little bear from the Pohutakawa Tree Series. The trunks of Pohutakawa trees grow in defiance of the winds and seas on the New Zealand coast.

DAWN NICHOLL
Grae Waki

DAWN HAS A fine arts background and exhibited her paintings before moving into sculpture. She was working with paper sculpture when she felt the need for a new direction and so took a course in felt-making. She expected to use felt as a sculptural material, but she fell into bear-making instead, and in 1987 participated in her first doll shows.

Possibly unique in the bear world, Dawn's bears are hand-moulded in coloured felts. Originally Dawn used river rocks as moulds but now she makes the mould first and then shapes her bear over it. She works in series, which sometimes take up to two years to complete, and all her bears are one-offs. Her work has been covered by many international bear books and magazines.

Her Grae Wakis are usually 30 cm (12") to 50 cm (20"), but have ranged from 5 cm (2") to over a metre (3 ft). All her bears, including the small furry bears are labelled with a blue woven cloth tag attached under the right arm. (On early bears her tag was on the outside of the arm.) Dawn enjoys making small furry bears as well, 'for light relief' as she puts it. She calls these Bidibids, and also sells some of them directly and at exhibitions and shows.

Dawn teaches her unique way of bear-making with felt as well as the traditional method. She believes that the ideal bear 'must be capable of looking directly at you. It must appear to be alive, but fozen in a moment.'

Dawn sees her work as sculptural pieces for adults, to be viewed as works of art. Her bears are certainly some of the most original in the bear artist world today.

Dawn Nicholl

ROBIN RIVE

Countrylife New Zealand

ROBIN HAD NEVER had a teddy bear as a child and in 1980 she was determined to remedy the situation. Before beginning her bear business, Robin had been involved in many aspects of design. She designed one-off women's dresses and sportswear, and also her present home, a 16th-century-style Japanese house and garden.

From the first few bears, Robin's bear-making quickly grew into a large business, and is now the largest bear-making company in Australia and New Zealand. Robin now employs about 80 people, exports her bears to 10 countries and participates in up to 20 shows around the world each year.

Robin's bears are mostly inspired by the early traditional styles and are given a pre-loved look by a unique four-stage process. They come in a range of sizes from 15 cm (6") to over 60 cm (24"), in both acrylic and mohair. Each bear has Robin's signature on the footpad, a signature on the label and personalised Limited Edition certificates.

Robin's bears have appeared in many bear and general publications. Several have been photographed on their world travels and will soon appear in a book and a series of postcards. In the year 2000 Robin plans to hold a Teddy 2000 Festival at her farm, and is designing a range of eco-Earth Love Bears, with part of the proceeds to go towards helping disadvantaged children.

Clockwise from left: Sean, 18 cm (7"), with hand-knitted arran scarf and tammy hat; Clancy, 32 cm (14"), with green shamrock waistcoat and glasses; Rafferty, 43 cm (17"), in hat and scarf; Paddy, 43 cm (17"), in shamrock waistcoat and glasses; Brady, 40 cm (16"), in arran sweater; Kelly, 18 cm (7"), in green felt with shamrock; and Joe, 15 cm (6"), in arran sweater. All in acrylic.

Standing: Chesterton, 43 cm (17"), with Algernon and Matilda, both 32 cm (14"); and little Num Num, 12 cm (4¾"). All in synthetic fabrics.

Robin Rive with Chesterton, 43 cm (17"), in vintage acrylic with waistcoat and glasses.

A group of Rayna's small bears, from 6 cm (2½") to 16 cm (6¼"), in mohair and velvet. All hand-stitched.

RAYNA SHONE

Ray-Beth Bears

*I*N 1980 RAYNA made a bear for her grandchild and her bear-making grew from there, fuelled by friends wanting bears for their children and grandchildren. Before she knew it, Rayna found herself selling bears at doll shows. It wasn't until 1987, however, when she moved to Tauranga, that Rayna started to think of herself as a serious bear-maker.

Although she has no formal training, Rayna has long been interested in crafts, and started embroidery and sewing when she was 10 years old. She makes all her bears alone in what is a full-time occupation for her. In 1994 she sold 150 bears. Rayna makes bears in all sizes, but she prefers them under 16.5

cm (6½"). She hand-sews these little ones. The bears are evolving their own look, and Rayna finds she is moving away from her earlier soft, plump bears towards a slimmer bear with longer arms. Each Ray-Beth Bear is sold with an identification card giving its details.

Ray-Beth Bears have won prizes in several shows, but Rayna admits that she lacks a competitive streak and therefore does not enter many competitions. She attends four shows around New Zealand each year, and finds that bear people are always very friendly. The only problem she has encountered lies in finding interesting materials to work with. She teaches bear-making classes and always encourages her students by telling them that the more bears they make, the better they will get.

Rayna gets great pleasure from making bears and hopes that her work

brings pleasure to her bears' new owners. Her aim is to travel overseas in order to experience more of the bear world.

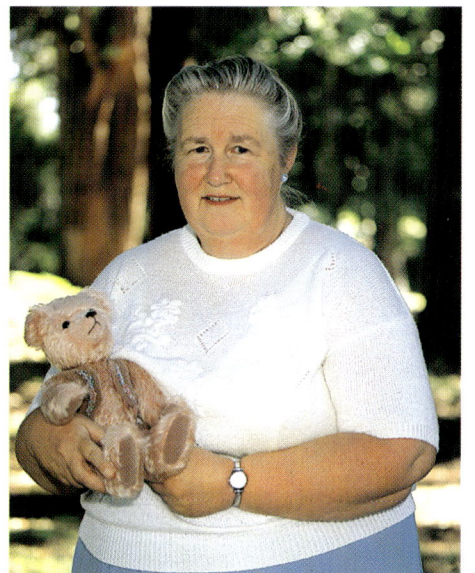

Rayna holding one of her bears.

Bear-making Supplies

When calling any of the Australian suppliers listed below, remember that an extra (eighth) digit is being phased in for telephone and fax numbers, starting with the prefix 9 in northern Sydney. Check with your telephone company if you have difficulties getting through.

Ron and Elke Block
Edinburgh Imports Inc.
PO Box 722
Woodland Hills
CA 91365-0722
US Fax. 0011 1 (818) 591 3806

Huge range of fabrics and accessories. Catalogue and samples available, international mail-order service, credit cards accepted.

Marlene De Lorenzo
Teddy's Bits Pty Ltd
PO Box 526
Gisborne VIC 3437

Mail-order fabrics, including German mohair, French and Australian acrylics. Classes taught.

Deirdre and Doug Glossop
Dee Glossop Teddy Bears & Accessories
86 Model Farms Road
Winston Hills NSW 2153
Ph./Fax. (02) 686 1682

Mohairs and synthetics, kits, patterns, accessories etc. Mail-order service, credit cards accepted. Catalogue available, showroom open to the public. Workshops taught, and restoration work taken.

Anne-Marie Hofman
Bears on Broadway
PO Box 81
Bangor NSW 2234
Ph./Fax. (02) 543 8937

Hand-dyed mohair, mini kits, miniature fabrics, patterns, old lace, books and accessories. Classes taught. International mail-order service, credit cards accepted.

Jennifer Laing
Totally Bear
6 Walter Road
Ingleside NSW 2101

The Art of Making Teddy Bears book and video and mohair kits available by mail order. Private classes, and restoration work taken on commission.

Heather Lyell
Bear Essentials
64 Dominion Road
Balmoral, Auckland, New Zealand
(PO Box 96120, Balmoral)
Ph./Fax. (09) 630 8479

For all your teddy bear requirements. Open six days a week. Evening classes taught.

Cindy McDonald
Beary Cheap Bear Supplies
PO Box 896
Mudgee NSW 2850
Ph. (063) 733 561
Fax. (063) 733 421

Large range of English and German mohair, alpaca, synthetics, kits, patterns etc. Mail-order service to Australia and New Zealand. Credit cards accepted. Catalogue and sample packs available. Wholesale enquiries welcome.

Adele Rowe
The Serendipity Collection
970 Mt Dandenong Tourist Road
Montrose VIC 3765
Ph./Fax. (03) 728 1979

Wide range of workshops, supplies, kits, miniatures and accessories, including country dolls, fairies and collectables.

Gerry Warlow
Gerry's Teddy & Craft Designs
30 John Street
Rosewood QLD 4340
Ph. (074) 641 843

Large range of mohair and synthetics, eyes, joints, kits etc. Catalogue and samples available. Credit cards accepted. Workshops taught.

Index of Artists

Helen Ackroyd
My Bear
5 Glenwood Avenue
Helena Valley WA 6056

Katherine Alam
Bondi Beach Bears
47 Glenayr Avenue
Bondi Beach NSW 2026

Linda Benson
Benson Bears
PO Box 251
Kurrajong NSW 2758

Anne Booth
Chadwick Bears
22 Koromiko Road
Wanganui NZ

Simone Burke
Bears by Simone
PO Box 193
Milsons Point NSW 2061

Ines Cook
What Ho Bears
19 Clarence Street
Blackwood SA 5051

Sandy Coombs
Sandy's Bears
'Ailsa', RD 54
Kimbolton NZ

Linda Davidson
Bramble Bears
PO Box 13
Mt Lawley WA 6050

Marlene De Lorenzo
Grubby Bears
PO Box 526
Gisborne VIC 3437

Samantha Fredericks
Bliss Toys
9 Lancaster Avenue
Newtown VIC 3220

Dawn Gibbon
Busselton Bears
8A Egret Close
Busselton WA 6280

Dee Glossop
Dee Glossop Teddy Bears & Accessories
86 Model Farms Road
Winston Hills NSW 2153

Helen Godfrey
Buzzbee Bears
82 Roden Street
West Melbourne VIC 3003

Ronwyn Graham
Bambini Design
PO Box 18
East Bentleigh VIC 3165

Loris Hancock
Studio Seventy
63 Woodgee Street
Currumbin QLD 4223

Jan Hanlon
Jan Hanlon Original Bears
Lot 6 Bradys Lookout
Rosevears TAS 7277

Judith Hardy
Lancewood Bears
29 Glen Terrace
Otumoetai, Tauranga NZ

Rhonda Harland
Booalbyn Bears
PO Box 131
Campbelltown NSW 2560

Janis Harris
Almost South Pole
PO Box 61126
Otara, Auckland NZ

Lexie Haworth
The Bears of Haworth Cottage
7 Walsh Crescent
North Nowra NSW 2540

Sharon Helleur
Blue Mountain Bears
PO Box 490
Springwood NSW 2777

Sonya Heron
Heartfelt Bears
13 Acqueduct Avenue
Mt Evelyn VIC 3796

Jane Higgins
Straw Beary Designs
97 Cavendish Street
Nundah QLD 4012

Rose Hill
Rose Hill Bears
PO Box 9592
Newmarket, Auckland NZ

Jan Hobart
Gaza Grizzlies
'Gaza'
Deniliquin NSW 2710

Marianne Howe
Omi's Bears
PO Box 38
Franklin TAS 7113

Carlene Hughes
Honey Pot Bears
46 Worthing Avenue
East Doncaster VIC 3109

Sharyn and David Hutchins
Brookside Bears
PO Box 571
Rosny Park TAS 7018

Michelle and Julie Hyland
Hyland Bears – Australia
PO Box 16
Kalamunda WA 6076

Christina Jackson
Sticky Paws
PO Box 278
Mornington VIC 3931

Mena Johnson
PO Box 274
Mosman NSW 2088

Lorraine Keen
Individual Bears
29 Gazania Road
Faulconbridge NSW 2776

Shirley Kerr
Penny Bears
5/41- 45 Sutherland Street
Cremorne NSW 2090

June Kittlety
Bear Fantastique
32 The Jinker Track
Albany Creek QLD 4035

Jennifer Laing
Totally Bear
6 Walter Road
Ingleside NSW 2101

Heather Lyell
D'Lyell Bears
PO Box 96–120
Balmoral, Auckland NZ

Sylvana McAuliffe
Sylvana's Miniature Bears
PO Box 212
Alstonville NSW 2477

Pol Dominic McCann
Mitchell Tyrie, Australian-made Bears
PO Box 1400
Collingwood VIC 3066

Cindy McDonald
Jumbuk Bears Pty Ltd
PO Box 896
Mudgee NSW 2850

Frances McLeary
Braidwood Bears
'Braidwood', Howden Road
RD 9 Frankton NZ

Rosalie MacLeman
MacBears
RSD T15
Woodstock-on-Lodden VIC 3109

Karla Mahanna
Karla Mahanna Artist Bears
16 Berwick Place
Greenvale VIC 3089

Fay Maloney
Fay M Bears
2/96 Carnarvon Street
East Victoria Park WA 6101

Margaret Ann Mann
Un Petit Bear – The Bear to Wear
9 Kalang Avenue
Killara NSW 2071

Carole Marshall
Balmain Bear
41 Wortley Street
Balmain NSW 2041

Kathleen Mason
Twink Bear Design
GPO Box 2475
Sydney NSW 2001

Denise Matthews
Denise & Friends Original Bears
PO Box 203
Diamond Creek VIC 3089

Margaret Michel
Original Bears by Margaret Michel
PO Box 461
Cockatoo VIC 3781

Collette Mitrega
Bow Bears Pty Ltd
176 Shepherds Drive
Cherrybrook NSW 2126

Gloria Morley
Belly-Button Bears
27 Seventh Avenue
Campsie NSW 2194

Syndi Muir
Muir Bears
c/o Akaroa Postal Service
Akaroa, Banks Peninsula NZ

Patricia Mullins
34 Gore Street
Fitzroy VIC 3065

Sara Murray
Bear Looms
53 Wanganui Avenue
Herne Bay, Auckland NZ

Judi Newman
Art Bears
PO Box 163
Gladstone QLD 4680

Dawn Nicholl
Grae Waki
40 Ross Street
Onerahi, Whangerei NZ

Elaine Pearce
Sheltons Original Bears
3 Pacific Way
Bathurst NSW 2795

Susan Priest
Paw Relations
PO Box 326
Cronulla NSW 2230

Glenys Ramage
Down to the Woods
16 Brookvale Avenue
Brookvale NSW 2100

Maria Riedl
The Riedl Bear Collection
PO Box 1984
Mildura VIC 3502

Robin Rive
Countrylife New Zealand
58 Elizabeth Knox Place
Auckland 6 NZ

Romy Roeder
Vagabond Bears, by Romy
PO Box 22
Lawson NSW 2783

Jenny Round
Round-A-Bout Bears
6 Kanahooka Street
Albion Park Rail NSW 2527

Adele Rowe
The Serendipity Collection
970 Mt Dandenong Tourist Road
Montrose VIC 3765

Debbie Sargentson
Nostalgia Bears
44 Ivanhoe Grove
Chadstone VIC 3148

Jennifer Shaw
Lairdswood Bears
14 Samuel Foster Drive
South Penrith NSW 2750

Rayna Shone
Ray-beth Bears
1/293 Levers Road
Tauranga NZ

Athans Steffen
Steffen Bears
55 Tucker Road
Moorabbin VIC 3189

Karen Stewart
Wern Dantsey Farm Bears
PO Box 1113
Chatswood NSW 2057

Pat Tomlinson
Oz-Born Bears
PO Box 3192
Parramatta NSW 2150

Kay VanderLey
Completely Stuf'd
204 Crotty's Lane
Kempsey NSW 2440

Bob White
Bob's Bears
PO Box 79E
East Devonport TAS 7310

Helen Williams
Bear-Foot Bears
PO Box LP-11
Lalor Park NSW 2147

Lyn Wilson
Lyn's Tiny Corner
4 Durunder Lane
Peachester QLD 4519

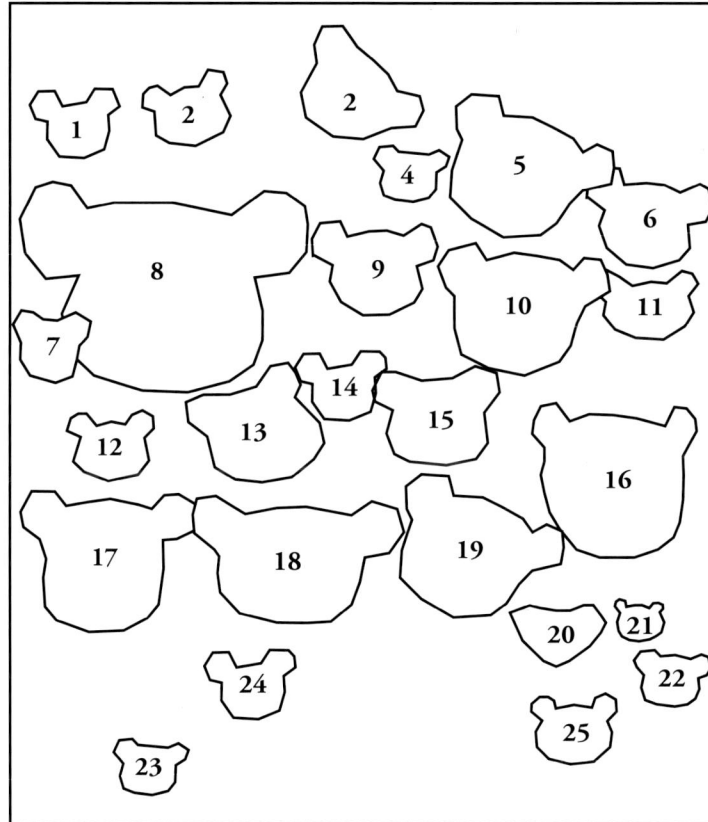

Front Cover Credits

1. Michelle and Julie Hyland, Hyland Bears – Australia, 30 cm (12"), in distressed beige mohair.
2. Denise Matthews, Denise & Friends Original Bears, 'Old Ted', 36 cm (14"), in distressed and sparse mohair.
3. A 1909 Steiff owned by the author, named Wilbur, 40 cm (16").
4. Jennifer Laing, Totally Bear, Geoffrey, 23 cm (9"), in golden tan mohair.
5. Carole Marshall, Balmain Bear, 60 cm (24"), in gold mohair with vest, collar, tie and glasses.
6. Kay Vanderley, Completely Stuf'd, Tavish, 36 cm (14"), in caramel mohair.
7. Pat Tomlinson, Oz-Born Bears, Scruffy, 15 cm (6"), in recycled fur.
8. Cindy McDonald, Jumbuck Bears Pty Ltd, Bartholemew, 78 cm (31"), in antique curly gold mohair.
9. Jennifer Laing, Totally Bear, Montgomery, 30 cm (12"), in honey mohair.
10. Jennifer Laing, Totally Bear, George, 46 cm (18"), in curly beige mohair, 1995 Golden Teddy Award nominee.
11. Adele Rowe, The Serendipity Collection, Bearly Old, 30 cm (12"), in sparse beige mohair.
12. Jennifer Laing, Totally Bear, Wilf, 18 cm (7"), in old gold mohair.
13. Jennifer Laing, Totally Bear, Woodruff, 36 cm (14"), in silver-tipped mohair.
14. Marianne Howe, Omi's Bears, Wellington, 15 cm (6"), in gold mohair.
15. Shirley Kerr, Penny Bears, 25 cm (10"), in pale gold mohair.
16. Romy Roeder, Vagabond Bears, by Romy, 50 cm (20"), in pale gold, blue and red mohair.
17. Shirley Kerr, Penny Bears, 25 cm (10"), in distressed tan mohair.
18. Karla Mahanna, Karla Mahanna Artist Bears, Old Girl with doll, 40 cm (16"), in sparse distressed tan mohair and tea-dyed cotton dress.
19. Athans Steffen, Steffen Bears, Hayfey, L/E 25, 42 cm (17"), in distressed gold mohair.
20. Pat Tomlinson, Oz-Born Bears, 30 cm (12"), an open-mouth bear in recycled fur coat.
21. Adele Rowe, The Serendipity Collection, 7.5 cm (3"), in beige mohair.
22. Linda Benson, Benson Bears, 13 cm (5"), in beige mohair with smocked playsuit, leather shoes, red wagon and tiny bear friend.
23. Mena Johnson, Panda, 10 cm (4"), in black and white synthetic.
24. Michelle and Julie Hyland, Hyland Bears – Australia, 15 cm (6"), in distressed beige mohair with bell collar.
25. Shirley Kerr, Penny Bears, 15 cm (6"), in ivory mohair.

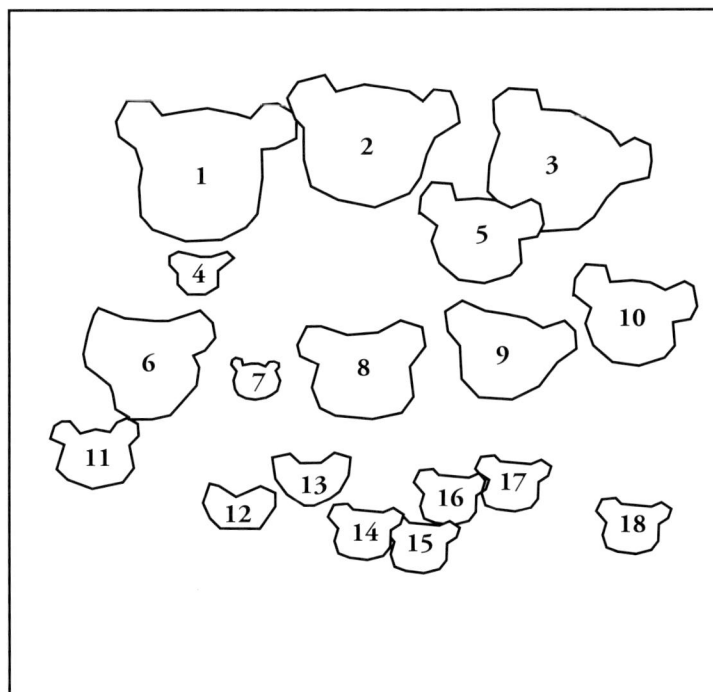

Back Cover Credits

1. Pat Tomlinson, Oz-Born, Scruffy, L/E 25, 15 cm (6''), in recycled fur.
2. Marianne Howe, Omi's Bears, Wellington, 15 cm (6''), in gold mohair.
3. Jennifer Laing, Totally Bear, Eddie, 15 cm (6''), in long sparse mohair.
4. Mena Johnson, Panda, 7.5 cm (3''), in upholstery velvets.
5. Jennifer Laing, Totally Bear, Gemma, 10 cm (4''), in mohair.
6. Michelle and Julie Hyland, Hyland Bears – Australia, 15 cm (6''), in shaggy mohair with bell collar.
7. Lyn Wilson, Lyn's Tiny Corner, Cranston John, 7.5 cm (3''), in upholstery velvet with collar and tie.
8. Shirley Kerr, Penny Bears, 15 cm (6''), in ivory mohair.
9. Linda Benson, Benson Bears, Teddy's Walk, 13 cm (5''), in mohair with smock and shoes.
10. Jennifer Laing, Totally Bear, Baby Alice Springs the Kangaroo, 11.5 cm (4½''), in mohair.
11. Marianne Howe, Omi's Bears, Dover, 7.5 cm (3''), in sparse gold mohair.
12. Adele Rowe, The Serendipity Collection, 7.5 cm (3''), in mohair.
13. Linda Benson, Benson Bears, Buckshot Bear, 7.5 cm (3''), in distressed cotton.
14. Margaret Ann Mann, Un Petit Bear – The Bear to Wear, Little Swagman, 6.5 cm (2½''), in suede with outfit.
15. Mena Johnson, Lily, 6.5 cm (2½''), in upholstery velvet with lace ruff.
16. Adele Rowe, The Serendipity Collection, Tally, 7.5 cm (3''), a pyjama bear with blanket.
17. Linda Benson, Benson Bears, 2.5 cm (1''), jointed teddy toy in wagon for Teddy's Walk.
18. Lyn Wilson, Lyn's Tiny Corner, 5 cm (2''), jointed, in white felt.